The Disciple and Economy

Additional works in this series include:

The Nature of The Soul

Creative Thinking

The Soul and Its Instrument

Leadership Training

Printed editions of some of the above works are
available through Wisdom Impressions.

II

The Disciple and Economy

By Lucille Cedercrans

Wisdom Impressions
Whittier, CA

The Disciple and Economy
by Lucille Cedercrans

First edition, 2002

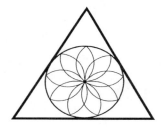

Wisdom Impressions is a group of practitioners of The Wisdom. Our purpose is to help create the appearance, support the teaching, and facilitate the distribution of The Wisdom.

Wisdom Impressions
P.O. Box 6457
Whittier, CA 90609-6457

ISBN 1-883493-26-9

IV

The Great Invocation

From the point of Light within the Mind of God
Let light stream forth into the minds of men.
Let Light descend on Earth.

From the point of Love within the Heart of God
Let love stream forth into the hearts of men.
May Christ return to Earth.

From the center where the Will of God is known
Let purpose guide the little wills of men —
The purpose which the Masters know and serve.

From the center which we call the race of men
Let the Plan of Love and Light work out
And may it seal the door where evil dwells.

Let Light and Love and Power restore the Plan on Earth.

"The above Invocation or Prayer does not belong to any person or group but to all Humanity. The beauty and the strength of this Invocation lies in its simplicity, and in its expression of certain central truths which all men, innately and normally accept — the truth of the existence of a basic Intelligence to Whom we vaguely give the name of God; the truth that behind all outer seeming, the motivating power of the universe is Love; the truth that a great Individuality came to earth, called by Christians, the Christ, and embodied that love so that we could understand; the truth that both love and intelligence are effects of what is called the Will of God; and finally the self-evident truth that only through *humanity* itself can the Divine Plan work out."

Alice A. Bailey

V

Editor's Foreword

The Disciple and Economy is part of a series of works on the path of self-initiated spiritual growth and development. These works are designed to facilitate step-by-step unfoldment from individuality to group awareness and conscious service to the One Life. This conscious service is called the path of discipleship, and those who walk this path are called Disciples.

The previously published books in the series include: *The Soul and Its Instrument, Creative Thinking,* and *The Nature of the Soul.* These texts are the basic training manuals for all of the work that follows. Their essential purpose is to organize, discipline, and develop the soul-mind-brain alignment of the disciple. This is accomplished through a progressive series of meditation exercises and practices (as particularly described in *The Nature of the Soul*). Since the main thrust of the work is along Seventh Ray lines, the emphasis is on "learning through application" rather than study. This means that to the degree one practices the meditations one comes to understand the meaning of the work.

A fourth textbook entitled *The Disciple and Economy* was planned and started. This work was to be the first in a new series, designed for those who had completed the earlier training and were becoming practitioners of The Wisdom and servants of the One Life.

Unfortunately, the new series was never finished. The only portion that exists is the "Introductory" lesson of *The Disciple and Economy.* Fortunately, Lucille left other materials on the subject.

Lucille described the method used to create the materials in the following extract from an unpublished class:

"Well, in the first place, Masters don't write the lesson material. I write it. They don't determine the words that will be used. I determine the words that will be used. They have taken those principles of truth which are incorporated in the lesson material and placed them, put them into abstract thought-forms. Now, these abstractions are above the level of words, they are above the frequency of pictures. They are in the frequency of meaning itself.

"Now, for instance, ... I as the station am using the English language and let's say that there is a station using the French language, one using the Russian language and so on. We don't contact these thought-forms via words. We contact the meaning. A Master does not speak to us via the written word or the formulated word. Even in individual instruction or group instruction such as this, we do not receive that instruction ourselves in word form. We receive the instruction as abstract concepts, meaning, It is a transference of ... meaning which includes a vast field of knowledge. We receive that transference of ... meaning into our consciousness and there in meditation we have to interpret that meaning and to translate it into whatever language we are using, and ... of course each language has its own advantages and its own disadvantages in interpreting and translating these concepts.

"Some languages are very difficult. In some areas, for instance, the English is most difficult ... because there are some meanings that we don't have words for. Our language simply hasn't gone into these areas of meaning, so that there is no word formulated that will convey the meaning, and it is at times very difficult to find the right assemblage of words, to carry the meaning and give it expression."

Lucille Cedercrans, Oct. 1, 1960

When Lucille spoke without a text, using the above technique, her presentations were commonly taped and transcribed. Thirty-three of these transcribed presentations were on subjects related to economy and finance. The transcripts of these presentations (minus the student questions and comments) constitute the bulk of the following work.

These verbal presentations were not originally designed for the written form. The editors have made a few small changes, but the meaning, quality, and style of the original transcripts remain intact.

The Masters

As Lucille's explanation makes clear, she, herself, translated a *frequency of meaning* into words. Since she translated that frequency into first-person-singular speech, it appeared as though another being was speaking. This was not actually the case. The words are in fact Lucille's. With that understanding, the frequencies identified include:

Master R, the head of the Seventh Ray Ashram. As such, he is in charge of the motion of Divine Intent into form, also known as Divine Law and Order, or Ceremonial Magic. Unless otherwise stated, the frequency translated is that identified as "Master R".

The Mahachohan or "Lord of Civilization" is one of the three highest offices of the Spiritual Hierarchy. This office is held by the Master or head of the Third Ray Ashram. At the time of these presentations, both of these offices were held by the Master R.

"The Master John is a disciple of the 5th degree, though he has not completed the ascension. He is working

VIII

along Seventh Ray lines and has been close to Me (Master R) for a long period of time. While He is working primarily with Seventh Ray, His nature is peculiarly Second. So, it is this combination of the Second and the Seventh Ray that He brings to you. You will find that His methods will be quite different from those of Mine. However, I give My approval and give Him My support."

Studying The Disciple and Economy

Master R:

I would like to make a few suggestions, which will, if carried out, render this intensive training period more easily completed.

The greatest difficulty with which you are faced as you enter into a training of this kind, is the problem of continuity and absorption. This is an intensive training, during which you will receive many concepts, experience many expansions of consciousness which come so quickly and closely together that there appears to be very little time for proper absorption and evaluation of projected instruction.

Therefore, it is vitally important that as you enter into this new phase of growth, you do so with the realization that the experiences which will be yours during this period will differ greatly from those experiences in learning which have gone before.

In order to avoid cycles in which you are hampered with mental indigestion, attempt to move with the energy flow of the activity. Receive the concept as it is projected, attempt to understand that concept as your consciousness is expanded to understand it, and then for the moment relegate that concept to the subconscious to be absorbed below the threshold of your awareness. Do not worry the concept after it has been projected and your attention is directed to a new concept. This is most important.

If at any time you feel that you are receiving more than you can absorb, more than you can understand at the moment, then refer back to this instruction. Relegate all that has gone before to the subconscious to be absorbed below the threshold of your awareness. Realize as you do so that the greatest degree of activity, insofar as this training is concerned, will take place below the threshold of your awareness. That which you are conscious of at the moment is but a minor indication of the changes which are taking place within the sum total of your consciousness.

Table of Contents

XIV

INTRODUCTORY

Every disciple who stands upon the threshold of world
service, regardless of how small may be the part he will
play in that activity, is faced with the necessity to
know, to understand, and to wield the Economy of the
One Life. He must grasp it as a Divine Plan in itself. He
must see its relationships within the affairs of humanity, and come to understand its laws so well as to be
enabled always to apply it to the furtherance of the
evolutionary plan of the Soul.

What stand does the disciple take in the conflict between the two major ideologies of our time? And more
important, why does he take that stand? What are his
views regarding cartels, monopolies, cooperatives, small
business, socialism, free trade, coexistence; and from
what perspective are these views formulated? Does he
understand the laws which govern the circulation of the
world's resources, and in that understanding can he see
the network of relationships necessary to the working
out of The Plan of Love and Light for humanity? What
does right use, right activity, and right planning mean
to him in relationship to economy? What does economy
itself mean to him?

These are questions which the trainee disciple can seldom answer clearly without giving way to emotional-
ism. He reacts to them from the persona level rather
than formulating a response from the level of Soul idea-
tion. Most trainees and many probationers avoid formulating an answer to such questions because they do not
understand the issues involved between universal principles and the selfish interests of the separated power
groups in the world. Yet before the disciple can play

1

The Disciple and Economy

even a small part in a world service activity, he must have resolved the problems of understanding which these questions arouse within him, so that he is clear in his vision and able to discriminate between the important and the lesser important.

This series of instructions clearly outlines The Divine Plan for humanity in its economic aspect. It shows those new economic forms upon which the new civilization can be safely constructed, and by which the Purpose of God can be demonstrated through Humanity. It withholds nothing from the open eye of the disciple, in the economic sense, that will enable him to throw his weight upon the side of Light in the struggle now ensuing between the forces of Light and the forces of darkness upon this planet. It is written in an endeavor to give the modern disciple, in whatever nation, position, or circumstance he may be placed, a basic understanding of the Economy of the One Life and Its Laws, so that he may serve The Plan justly and wisely in the world of mankind.

It is presumed that any disciple entering upon a study of this kind will have embodied within himself the concepts and energies of good will, loving understanding, and service to one's fellow man, all of which result in right human relations. These are prerequisite to participation in a world service activity which is set into motion from hierarchical levels and inspired by those Great Lives Whose Love for humanity far surpasses anything known on the planet today.

Embodiment of the concepts and energies of good will, loving understanding, and service to one's fellow man is the first step along the Path of Discipleship. Embodiment of the instruction following in this treatise is the second step. The third and final step is taken in active service to The Plan as the disciple lives, moves, and has his being within the body of humanity.

2

Introductory

The Economy of the One Life is an organization of the energy, force, and substance of Its many parts into that divine activity which serves the evolution of the total. In Its highest aspect as a Cosmic Law, It establishes and maintains that relativity of interchange and exchange which is the circulatory Life of the ordered Cosmos.

This great Cosmic Law works out within our Solar system via three subsidiary laws about which little can be said at this time. Suffice it to say that:

1. The Law of Free Circulation establishes the rhythmic ebb and flow of the energy, force, and substance of the system throughout the totality, so that the part may partake of that of which it is aware. This law provides equal opportunity to every organized life within the system, via an ebb and flow of all energy, force, and substance through the etheric web which is the integrated, substantial, and substantive body of the Solar Logos. This web, resembling a vast network of arteries and veins or a huge nervous system, interpenetrates every form and the so-called space between the forms of the system, providing the medium through which the Omnipresence of God is made manifest. More will be said about this later on in the series.

2. The Law of Harmonious Placement arranges, according to color and tone, every life in relationship to every other life and the Central Directing Will of the system. It sets up the basis of relativity of one body to another; of one consciousness to another; of one organized life to another, impelling those relationships to serve the Divine Purpose of the total.

3. The Law of Formulation establishes and controls

3

the constant motion of substance to reflect the steady evolution of consciousness, thereby producing in the phenomenal world the needed forms through a ceaseless inner destructive and constructive activity which we see and know as change.

These Solar Laws are stepped down upon our planet into three basic laws of Economy which have to be worked out and applied by humanity (the brain of the Planetary Logos) within its life and affairs. Thus, the Planetary Logos waits upon humanity and its evolution, just as the Solar Life waits upon Him.

These three Planetary Laws relate specifically with three aspects or phases of intelligent activity: the first having to do with the intelligent activity of purpose or direction, the second having to do with the intelligent activity of consciousness, and the third having to do with the intelligent activity of substance.

Each of the three laws brings these great occult principles into active play within the life and affairs of man. Thus, when the whole of the Law of Economy is applied, nine occult principles of great significance in the Purpose and Plans of the Logos are invoked into activity.

We shall first enumerate the Laws and Principles involved, and then move on to a definition and explanation of each.

1. The Law of Right Use

   a. The Principle of Sharing

   b. The Principle of Supply and Demand

   c. The Principle of Democratic Participation in the One Life

Introductory

A. THE LAW OF RIGHT USE

This is the first phase of intelligent activity having to do with the directional Will of God in substance and the invocation of the Power aspect of Deity. It brings the following occult principles into active play in the three worlds of human endeavor.

1. The occult Principle of Sharing which is based upon the Fatherhood of God and the Brotherhood of Man. This great principle is born out of the fact in nature that all Life is a One Life, and that the part has equal share in the energy, force, and substance of that Life.

The kingdoms in nature share with one another the life-giving substance of the planet. Beyond this, human beings share with one another, far more than they now realize, the experiences of the one humanity. These experiences of so-called pain and pleasure, of loss and gain, of good and bad, produce the growth and development of human consciousness. They are basic in their universality. No one is left out of them. Each in his own

5

time shares in the experience of the other, so that behind the many separated forms, each with its focus of consciousness, there is an integrated, inner life which we call humanity.

Before we proceed, let each disciple pause and reestablish his interior, vertical alignment with pure Truth. Let him seek the revelation of that Truth, and stand steady in the Light of his own Soul, for the implications and ramifications of the above are tremendous in their impact upon the form nature of our modern world.

balance ✝

If one looks fearlessly at this great Principle of Sharing and is able to grasp its meaning with clarity, the following Truth emerges: that right use of that which we have, which is a basic law of economy, and without which a healthy economy is impossible, demands that every human being has the divine right to an equal share, according to his need, of the world's resources (its energy, force, and substance), the world's productivity (its forms), and the world's work (its activity).

supply precipitates demand

2. The occult principle that an abundant supply precipitates demand, and must therefore follow that formulated demand into outer appearance. This principle is based upon the fact in nature that every focus of consciousness is abundantly supplied with the energy, force, and substance out of which he may create the bodies and forms of experience which produce his growth and development as a Spiritual Son of God. He is supplied with mental, astral, and etheric substance; thus he demands an instrument of contact with the three lower worlds, and such an instrument makes its appearance in the light of day. He is supplied with the experience of humanity; therefore he demands such experiences, and they make their appearances in his daily life and affairs.

Introductory

A formulated demand — which, remember, is always precipitated by an abundant supply — takes its form in the consciousness of human beings as a need, a necessity of life. For instance, the abundance of electricity in our modern civilization has precipitated the formulated demand for so many of the forms of this age. In many parts of the world electric light has become one of the common necessities. Modern man needs light; therefore it follows his formulated demand into his home, his street, and his city.

There is an abundant supply of Truth overshadowing humanity which is precipitating within the brain consciousness of human beings everywhere the need to know Truth, which is the formulated demand for Its appearance. Thus, we are assured of a new dispensation, of great revelations in every school of thought and every department of human living as supply follows demand into specific manifestation.

This principle, when brought into related activity with the occult Principle of Sharing, establishes the basis of that sharing: Who shall have what — and when?

The answer is, of course, that the individual and the group shall have the supply which fulfills their need at the time of that need, and thus we come again to right use. Is it right use of the world's resources, and the world's productivity for one group of men to have more to eat than is good for the health and welfare of their bodies, while others go hungry? Can there possibly result from such use a healthy economy within which the masses can achieve the greatest growth and development?

I should like to make it clear at this moment that this treatise is not a condoning of the communist doctrine, nor will it suggest that the solution of this problem lies in the forceful taking from the rich in order to give to the poor. There is a solution, a divine activity into which disciples can enter, which will manifest The Divine Plan for humanity with a minimum of human suffering. Furthermore, that minimum will not be caused by armed forces, but by the individual's own insight into his share of cause for the world's problems. In other words, the only pain karmically necessary to him is that of seeing himself as a contributing part of humanity's criminal past. This burden of guilt will be expiated as the individual sets his affairs in order, i.e., as he helps to restore The Divine Plan on earth.

It is at this point that the concept of necessity must be reevaluated and redefined by men and women everywhere.

It must be borne in mind that the Purpose and Goal of Life on this planet is the growth and development of all consciousness imprisoned therein into its overshadowing, divine counterpart.

Human need, then, is for that which is conducive to such growth. It entails far more than the basic necessities of the physical body, though these do come first since they are so glaring in their lack of fulfillment. For so long as humanity permits any part of its brotherhood to live in poverty, while other parts live in wealth, it shall suffer the symptoms of its diseased circulatory system. These symptoms are communism, fascism, socialism, capitalism, etc., none of which is the true outpicturing of The Divine Plan in its economic aspect.

It is necessary to live the vision of the goal of human growth in order to truly define the level of necessity. In "The Nature of The Soul" that goal is clearly conveyed as the Conscious Soul Incarnate, with all that such a term connotes. What, then, is the level of necessity most conducive to such growth?

Introductory

All human beings should need, above and beyond the basic requirements for physical existence, an atmosphere within which the good qualities and characteristics within them can develop into full flower.

You will note I have used the terms "should need". It is the task of the disciple in the world today to bring the potential supply — potential fulfillment — into direct overshadowing, and then to help formulate a new demand in response to that overshadowing.

All men and women then "should need" freedom — equality of opportunity insofar as education, culture, creativity, beauty, and harmony are concerned — in order to achieve the greatest growth and development of their divine potential. Every human being, regardless of his point of development, "should need" to make his conscious contribution to a better world. Without the above equality of opportunity, he has little chance of doing so. Every man spiritually needs the security of Love, that Love which gave his Soul birth, and his humanity dominion over the earth and all of the Kingdoms below him in nature. Right use of such dominion would restore that security of Love to him.

> 3. The Principle of Democratic Participation in the affairs of the One Life, which is based upon the fact that God gave the individual man freedom of choice. This great occult principle to which so many in the world have responded actually brings into the area of world affairs a new frequency and a new blend of energies which are the precipitating factors of the New Age of the Soul.

In many places men and women and nations have responded to the democratic concept and are acting as conductors for the release of its energies into the affairs of humanity; but nowhere, as yet, has the pure truth of

The Disciple and Economy

this concept been brought into contact with the race-mind consciousness. It still remains to be understood with clarity, and embodied within any part of the mass consciousness and its instrumentality.

It must be remembered that humanity still finds itself at that point of evolution where selfish interests, backed by economic strength and the force of arms, are the supreme power. It commands the greatest focus of energy and therefore the greatest force; but its power is on the wane, though this fact is hardly perceptible at this time. Democracy is, as yet, an ideal and a word; while small but powerful groups, motivated by selfish interests, still rule the masses in greater or lesser degree throughout the world. These exert a powerful influence and a tremendous hold as they put up a last ditch opposition to the new impulse now coming in. The concept of equality is coming more and more to the fore; the humanitarian impulse is finding a response within the many hearts which are beating to a new and more inclusive rhythm. Thus the crisis of our times, evidenced by so much world unrest, comes into its own.

As the concept of democratic participation in the One Life begins to make its influence felt, it should clarify the concept of leadership, providing humanity with those leaders who will, through their ability to be inspired and in turn to inspire the masses, swing the governments of the world into a true democratic function.

When democracy is grasped by humanity as a divine truth, and applied in daily living, all men and women of maturity will hold an equal voice in the affairs of the community, the state, the nation, and the world. They will be adequately educated (not propagandized) to understand the issues of their times, and to contribute toward the solution of their common problems. The impartial, bipartisan, cooperative give-and-take of individuals, groups, and nations will help to bring in a new era of human success where right relationships will be the outstanding achievement of the age.

Democratic participation in the One Life implies also a democratic economy of, by, and for the people, where each partakes of and contributes to the world's abundant supply. This again is right use, right use of supply and that network of relationships through which supply is distributed among the people according to their needs.

Before such a manifestation of The Divine Plan is possible, the people themselves must take an interest in both their government and their right education. An education in the principles of a truly democratic civilization, with its particular culture and economy, must reach into the masses and evoke right action from them. Democracy entails responsibility, and right government begins with the self. When democracy is misused, it carries its own karmic consequences, the evidence of which can be seen in the world today. In the United States where the democratic concept is both an ideal and an excuse for separativeness, its wrong use has created many imprisoning forms within which the American people struggle for freedom. If man is to have freedom, he must make right use of such as he has. He must wield it toward the betterment of the total. One has only to look at the solidity of today's imprisoning forms, and the suffering of the human beings caught within them, to grasp the immensity of the task which lies ahead. Yet God gave man the freedom of choice. It has been through the use of such freedom that man has achieved his present growth and precipitated the present crisis in world affairs.

B. THE LAW OF RIGHT ACTIVITY

This law sets into motion the second phase of intelligent

The Disciple and Economy

activity. It brings the consciousness aspect into right action and evolves within it that Divine Love-Wisdom which in its essence is the very Soul of all that is. It brings the following occult principles into active play in the three planes of human endeavor:

1. The occult Principle of Individuality which is based upon the fact that while all consciousness is of the One Life, each focus of consciousness is:

   a. at a specific point of evolutionary development, and therefore individual in tone and color;

   b. a differentiated expression of the One Life, and therefore individually expressive of the One Purpose; and

   c. gifted with special talents and tendencies.

This occult principle means simply that every man and woman has a specific and peculiar relationship with and within the One Life which is one's own. Humanity is a brotherhood within which the individuality of each must be accepted, accounted for, and worked with, if the good of the whole is to be established and maintained. The total is composed of Individualities, each expressive of Purpose, Power, and Will, which only in their right relationship with one another can reflect the overshadowing Purpose, Power, and Will of God. Thus any doctrine or state which endeavors to swallow up the individual into a homogenous mass is false and will not stand the pressures of either evolution or human need. Any network of relationship must be founded upon the cooperative give-and-take of the individuals concerned if it is to carry the right activity of The Plan. There must be a willingness of each to be so related in order to provide a network via which the energies, forces, and substances of the One Life can be brought into right activity through the right action of the consciousness itself.

There is a specific activity which is right for each individual and which can only be determined by the individual himself as the society provides him with every opportunity of doing so. The society, then must eventually discover how to provide each with that which is most conducive to his growth.

The conductors of this aspect of The Plan into outer manifestation are:

a. the educational opportunities to develop the individual according to this present point of evolution and according to his talents and tendencies; plus the cultural atmosphere which sustains, evokes, and releases the individual expression of consciousness through its instrumentality;

b. the recognition of responsibility on the part of those whose present karma is such that they can aid in this effort.

The above provides each with the opportunity to enter into that activity which is right for him, and furthermore, it is a positive aid toward the discovery and acceptance by each of that activity within which he can best function. Right choice of one's field of activity, and of the part one can best play within that field, will then become a common manifestation rather than the rare occasion which it now is.

2. The occult Principle of Equality which is based upon the fact that each man, in his right and specific relationship with and within the One Life, is of vital importance to that Life. Thus, each man carries within himself the seed and pattern of greatness. Each is endowed with a

particular potential which is essential in the
working out of The Divine Plan for humanity;
thus the importance to the Whole of one, regardless of outer appearances, is as great as is the
importance of another. All men share equally in
the beauty, the harmony, and the perfection of
the One Life as that One Life manifests Its Plan
via the evolution of the human brotherhood
within itself.

The impact of this great occult principle upon the body
of humanity has created much confusion within the race
mind consciousness; for where in outer appearance is
there evidence of an equality among men? Men and
women do not appear to be born equal. The conditions
of their birth vary greatly, and all too often the opportunities afforded them are limited to those conditions
throughout a lifetime.

The very fact of evolution itself would seem to dispute
the concept of equality, for some are further evolved
than are others; hence their natural development would
tend to push the lesser evolved into a much less equal
position within the affairs of the One Life.

The student must lift his awareness far above the small
picture he sees in the present time and space to understand clearly the concept of equality.

The lesser evolved provide those who have gone before
them with their opportunity of growth, while the more
highly evolved do likewise for those who follow. Even
here there is a cooperative give-and-take, for the disciple could make no progress if it were not for his brothers. His evolution is achieved through his service to
humanity, his wise guidance, and care of those whose
awareness is less than his own. Thus, the manifestation
of The Divine Plan is as dependent upon one as it is
upon the other.

Introductory

You have heard it said that "the first shall be last, and the last shall be first." The meaning underlying this relates with the concept of equality. Regardless of how far along the Path the individual may be, he cannot take the final initiation into the One Life until all of his brothers stand ready with him; thus the first to reach this point of development must wait and serve until the last approaches. Occultly speaking, the serving initiate holds wide the door through which his younger brother passes.

    3.   The occult Principle of Grace which is based upon the Love of God in the sacrificial act of the Christ. The sacrificial act of the Christ means simply that this aspect of the One Life, this higher consciousness of Deity, deliberately and at great sacrifice, identifies with every human being in every condition and circumstance.

This great consciousness of Love deliberately gives Its awareness to man's violation and denial of that Love. There is no state or condition of consciousness too low or too degenerate for the Christ to live within. He takes on, via such identification, the sins, the guilts, the horrors of human action in order to insure man's growth up out of these into a Divine Light and Life. This great, acutely aware consciousness, which could in one moment of decision tune out the frequencies of that which is so foreign to its nature, never wavers but takes upon itself the suffering of man's inhumanity to man. Thus, not one human being, regardless of his action, is left out of the heart and mind of the Christ. Through the Principle of Grace, every man is assured of his divine place within the One Life.

The principle is a recognition that all consciousness is rooted in both so-called good and evil and will evolve along either path according to:

The Disciple and Economy

    a. the mass tendency;

    b. the present opportunity; and

    c. individual choice.

There is so much that takes place in the world today which the average occultist either blames or excuses as being the result of individual karma and choice. The careless, thoughtless, and little-knowing shrug of the shoulders which indicates "this is his karma", with no effort to adjust that karma, knows nothing of the Grace of the Christ. Such Grace supersedes individual karma via a Love that surpasses human understanding, providing the disciple with his opportunity and his obligation.

Through Grace, the loving, giving action of the Christ, all men are forgiven, and all cyclically receive a new opportunity for right growth. Such a cycle is upon us now where the individual can be given a new opportunity through the betterment of his environing situation and circumstances. Thus, the mass tendency is worked with and an effort is made to swing it into right activity. The society is reeducated and reconditioned, and begins to consciously take its proper place and responsibility in the shaping of individual destiny. The individual is forgiven his so-called sins in an understanding of the burden of racial, social, and national karma he is sharing with his brothers; and a way is provided whereby he can "go and sin no more."

Society presently sets its standards of acceptance, its rules of behavior, and fails on the most part to provide the opportunity whereby its untouchables can meet those standards or follow those rules. Society has a function to perform which it must discover if it is to serve The Divine Plan for humanity.

Introductory

There are those new social forms overshadowing and available today which would, if formulated and brought into objective manifestation, help man to achieve that growth in consciousness which is an adjustment of his karma. That such forms will create a certain amount of instability in the outer life and affairs of the present is true; but such conflict is the activity out of which harmony can be born. And do not forget, conflict is the evolutionary way of this planet. Let us begin to control the forces of conflict then, setting them into that motion which will produce the greatest rate of spiritual growth and development, or spiritual harmony, within the human family.

The invocation and application of Grace — of love and forgiveness — does tend to arouse opposition; but that opposition is a force which can be used in the working out of The Plan. More will be said anent this subject later on in the series.

Before we move our attention from the Law of Right Activity, it would be wise to consider the concept of group consciousness. The invocation of the three occult principles listed under this law, and their application in the life and affairs of humanity, directs the growth of the individual consciousness into that inter-relationship with other units of consciousness which evolves group awareness and group action.

Those disciples being trained in the world today, under the direction of the many ashrams active in a new and unprecedented educational effort, are receiving such training according to their subjective and objective group affiliation. The ashram works with the group consciousness via the Science of Impression. That which is to be impressed is turned to the group rather than to the individual; and according to his group awareness will he receive, absorb, and embody the concepts pouring down from the ashram into the three worlds of human endeavor. He makes his own individual relationship with Truth in accordance with his group place and function. Later in this series we shall consider the characteristics and qualities of group consciousness. In the meantime, much can be derived from meditation and contemplation upon the above.

C. THE LAW OF RIGHT PLANNING

This is the third phase of intelligent activity, having to do with the controlled motion of substance, and the invocation of the Divine Mind or Holy Spirit into influence in the outer life and affairs. It brings the following occult principles into active play within the body of humanity.

    1. The principle of Divine Prototype which is based upon the Holy Ghost aspect and Its formulation by the Christ into:

        a. the Angel of the Presence;

        b. The Divine Plan for humanity;

        c. the perfect form or pattern of manifestation for every Truth ideated by the Soul within the kingdom of God.

Truth exists before, above, and behind the Soul. It is the Spiritual Law, Nature, and Reality of Life. It is both general and specific, macrocosmic and microcosmic, and universal in its application.

The Soul ideates; i.e., he brings that quantity, quality, and strength of Truth, which he can grasp in his own meditative efforts, into idea form, thus stepping the macrocosmic down into the microcosmic, or the general into the specific, insofar as his level of awareness is concerned. The idea which is concrete and objective to

Plan for Your Life and
THRIVE

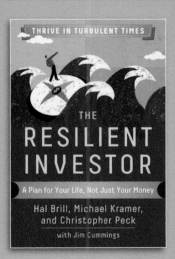

THRIVE IN TURBULENT TIMES

THE
RESILIENT
INVESTOR

A Plan for Your Life, Not Just Your Money

Hal Brill, Michael Kramer,
and Christopher Peck

with Jim Cummings

NATURAL INVESTMENTS LLC

www.naturalinvestments.com
www.resilientinvestor.com

THE
RESILIENT
INVESTOR

him then becomes the abstract reality, the higher concept of Truth toward which the man in the brain aspires.

The Holy Ghost aspect is the risen body (redeemed substance) of that total state of consciousness defined as
the Christ. It is the One Life within which the Lord
Maitreya and His Hierarchy of Masters live, move, and
have Their Being. Being composed of the finest frequency of intelligent substance toward which man can
reach, It is oft-times referred to as the Divine Mind. The
devic lives which make up this great and Divine Being,
for such It is even in Itself, are of a very high order; and
while they have been seen by many, and interpreted by
some as angels, saints, etc., they constitute in their sum
total the great Spiritual Mother of this planet.

Within the Mother, as within a great and perfect life-
giving planetary womb, the Father acting through His
Son, the Christ, plants His Seed; that is, here His Will
becomes visible as a perfect form of manifest expression. Such forms are called Divine Prototypes. They are
the vehicles already created to carry the perfected and
evolved Truth into appearance of activity. They are the
Spirit of Truth which guides the evolving consciousness
and form to its Divine conclusion. Thus, they overshadow the Spiritual Soul within the ashram.

From another perspective this aspect is that Light
within the Mind of God which we invoke into the minds
of men. Spiritual Light is both an appearance and a
quality of the Holy Ghost aspect. It is a radiation and a
forerunner of a higher form directly overshadowing the
disciple who meditates. The disciple who, in meditation,
receives the mental vision or impress of Light, can, if he
proceeds properly, penetrate beyond it to the Divine
Prototype producing it. In other words, the impress of
Light in meditation is an announcement of, as well as a
preliminary contact with:

a. the Soul;

b. the Angel of the Presence;

c. a Divine Prototype held in focus within the Mind of Christ.

2. The Principle of Relative Appearance which is based upon the fact that every Divine Prototype has its relative appearance within the body of humanity and its world of affairs. This is the meaning behind the occult statement, so often misunderstood and misinterpreted, "as above so below." Here is a "fact in nature" of such a tremendous spiritual significance that the awakened and intuitive disciple who seizes it will immediately see beyond the illusion and the glamour of appearance into the reality behind it. Every human form and the forms created by humanity are relative appearances of those Divine Prototypes which were made in the image of God and are the Divine Destiny and glory of mankind.

The disciple in meditation equates — i.e., finds the relationship between — the Divine Prototype and Its relative appearance in the world of affairs, thus clarifying the evolutionary growth to be achieved by the idea and consciousness incarnate within the imperfect form. Light is thrown upon the Path, and it is seen — no longer intuited, but seen — by the focused third eye. This is an "experience" which takes place in meditation and makes it possible for the disciple to formulate his service in an activity of right planning.

The forces of evolution respond to the relationship between the Divine Prototype and its relative appearance in the world of affairs, via a long slow process of trial and error until the disciple — the Conscious Soul Incarnate — can consciously wield those forces according to his vision of the growth to be made. Then the old way gives way to the new. The long slow process or path is forsaken for a speedier, more direct and realistic process of consciously initiated evolution.

3. The Principle of Sequential Change, which is based upon the fact that all growth is achieved through a series of sequential changes produced by the action of consciousness upon energy, force, and substance. When the consciousness "sees" the relationship between the higher and the lower, when he "sees" the path, as it were, he takes that relationship or path into his consciousness, where it is transferred directly as an impress or command into the economy of his own instrumentality. For instance, the relationship or path between the aspirant and the Divine Prototype, of which his vehicles and his integrated persona are a relative appearance, is the Conscious Soul Incarnate. That relationship — that path — is taken into the meditating consciousness where it is gradually and then finally "seen".

The action of the enlightened and evolving consciousness upon the mental energy, astral force, and etheric substance of his vehicles produces a series of experiences (sequential changes) which finally conclude the manifest expression and appearance of the Divine Prototype in the world of affairs. Thus, that evolution, which would otherwise have taken many thousands of incarnations to conclude, is focused into approximately three incarnations of ordered sequential changes. Once this path is initiated, every happening or change that the man in the brain experiences in his life and affairs narrows the gap between the Prototype and its appearance, The happening itself is meaningful; it, as a relative sequence of growth, is dynamic in its effects, regardless of how outwardly unimportant it may appear to be. Thus, the moment becomes the vehicle of eternity.

The Divine Plan for humanity in its economic aspect — i.e., the forms which will carry both the evolving and the evolved consciousness into appearance in the light of day — is held in solution as a vast prototype within the Mind of Christ. Here the lion and the lamb do lie down together, speaking in occult symbols.

Today, there are those within the Hierarchy Who, having equated a new relationship or path between the Prototype and its appearance in the world of affairs, are giving Themselves to a new effort for humanity. Together with a few of their senior disciples, They are forming the nucleus of a new Synthetic Ashram within which the Light, Love, and Power of God are being blended into a perfect synthesis which will precipitate the newly formulated relationship, or path, into the body of humanity. Once that new path is anchored within the human consciousness within the economy of its energy, force, and substance, and within its outer life and affairs, its evolution will be speeded up a thousandfold.

The nine occult principles, invoked into play by the application of the three basic laws of Economy, will bring rapid and sometimes drastic changes into the life and affairs of humanity. But each change will be a dynamic force for Spiritual growth and development.

It must be understood that the Synthetic Ashram, created out of a nucleus of the First, Second, and Seventh Ray Ashrams, does not presently supersede or outmode other more "tried and true", or more slowly moving efforts. These still persist, and are of greater strength within the Hierarchy than is the new one. Yet, if this experiment succeeds, it will be adopted by the entire Hierarchy in Its service to humanity during the next twenty-five-hundred-year cycle.

Certainly the methodology of the new effort differs greatly from that of others. Some of these differences are extremely important and the disciple either working within or aiding the Synthetic Ashram should endeavor to understand them. Here a few of these are enumerated and briefly explained:

1. The hierarchical approach to humanity is more direct and inclusive. While the Senior Disciple at hierarchical levels continues to work with humanity as a group life, he does, nonetheless, work directly with every level of development within that group life. Thus, the ashramic presentation of The Wisdom is formulated for, and has its application to, every state of consciousness from the heights to the depths of human development. It does not exclude those who do not "measure up", so to speak, but works with that state of consciousness which the man or woman is, where he is. The aspirant or the group of aspirants cannot "fall out of Grace" with his Senior, through any act, or series of acts, which are deemed unworthy. His acts will produce their karma, and more quickly than would otherwise be the case; but so long as he maintains his higher alignment and perseveres in his effort, regardless of the mistakes he makes, his new hierarchical focus will include him (as an evolving Son of God — a Soul) in Its attention.

The connotations of this are great and will undoubtedly cause much controversy within the field of discipleship itself. The aspirant, probationer, and disciple, working within the new ashram may not be a perfect example of The Wisdom, but they will be a perfect example of Its action or growth within the self-initiated evolutionary process.

The Disciple and Economy

The hierarchical experiment (for such it is) handles the opposition in a uniquely different and more functional way. The three masters who are responsible for the new Synthetic Ashram and Its efforts on behalf of humanity precognize the seeds of opposition within the presentation itself, its methodology and techniques, and relate or equate that opposition to its correspondence within the body of humanity and the world of affairs at any given moment. Then, working in cooperation with the Lords of Karma, They focus upon that related opposition through their service group in the world, evoking such opposition into appearance within the life and affairs of the group as a problem of humanity to be met and overcome in that specific time and place.

Preface

Evoking Opposition into Appearance
Within the Life and Affairs of a Service Group

In keeping with the Synthetic Ashram's new method of handling opposition, a portion of the ashramic group life incarnated with the seeds of opposition to The New Economy. They experienced and expressed all the problems with money, finance, organization, etc., that were then (and are now) typical of humanity and of those who aspire to serve the One Life.

After precipitating *The Nature of The Soul, Creative Thinking*, and other expressions of the New Thought-Form Presentation of The Wisdom, this group life (known as The Wisdom Group), was then called on to precipitate *The Disciple and Economy*. However, in order to bring this new work into appearance, they had first to transform their individual and group instrument. The application of essential techniques found in *The Nature of The Soul*, enabled them to deal with their embodied opposition to the new economy by realizing and manifesting that new economy, as a group, in their daily life and affairs.[1]

After some years of work, their efforts to manifest the new economy were derailed by the additional weight of external opposition. While only the Introductory lesson of *The Disciple and Economy* was precipitated, they did bring through a great deal of related information and

---

[1] For further indications regarding these essential skills, see *The Nature of the Soul Study Guide*, published by Wisdom Impressions.

25

The Disciple and Economy

techniques. This material on economy is gathered together for the first time in the following pages.

The Editors

Chapter 1

Old Forms

The Birth of the New,

Formulating the New Law,

The Search Light of the Soul

This teaching has been referred to as new, and yet it is as old as man himself. It has taken many forms as man has intuited it, and attempted to interpret it for those who were not yet ready to grasp it with the intuition. All of those forms have been right for the need of the time and place in which they made their appearance. That is the first thing man must recognize in his search for Truth; that all forms of teaching which came forth as a result of man's aspiration to God were inspired, that they were right for him at that time, that they fulfilled his need and made his growth into a greater realization of Truth possible. Do not, in your search, cast aside the old forms too quickly. Look within them, see and relate them to the need of their time, the Truth they contain, and soak up the essence of that Truth. Then the old outer form which has served its purpose can die a natural and painless death. Humanity will be released from its hold, released from the resentment and fear of it, and be left free to build a new form, free to mold that which will more perfectly reflect the new grasp and understanding of the same old Truth.

We live in a world today in which the new understanding is needed more than anything else, the new understanding which will balance the power of war and balance the power of fear, dread and hatred which produce war. We must bring to bear upon the daily life and affairs of our world the Power of Truth, so that man can know peace and in knowing it, live it.

The old forms have been mentioned here for a better understanding of the evolutionary process of the human consciousness. Many of them have served their purpose. They are ready to die, in fact, they are passing from us, and yet their going has produced such a struggle. We hold to them, cling to them, because we tend to fear the new. Man has been conditioned by the old forms and has become crystallized in them. Take for example, the man who could not follow Jesus because he had to remain behind and bury the dead. Jesus the Christ said to him, "Follow me and leave the dead to bury the dead." How many of those who have read His words have understood them? Man desperately needs to understand the Wisdom of His words, to be able to leave the old dead forms to the dead past and open his heart and mind to the birth of the new.

The teaching is not new, only its form is new and even that is so clearly related to the old that its understanding is simple.

I wish to speak with you very briefly regarding a subject of most importance and which provides another problem for the disciple. It is the sense of timing which is so necessary to the successful manifestation of any planned activity. The disciple is functioning under a different law than does the average man who sets out to accomplish any mental picture or plan.

As an example, the business man in the world today operates under known laws of the business world. Knowledge of these laws, understanding of them, are available to him through study, observation and very little experience. It is then only necessary for him to cooperate with those known laws in order to make of his business, barring karmic interference, a successful undertaking.

With the disciple, however, we find a much more subtle and therefore difficult situation manifesting. The disciple has no books to which he can refer which will equip him with knowledge of laws governing his actions in time and space. Because in the past there have been so few disciples, these laws are as yet unwritten, and I am not referring entirely to the written word, but to the fact in manifestation. The disciple has, in one sense, passed over from one world in which certain coordinates provide his limitations, his boundaries, his laws, making possible certain expressions into a world in which the new law is not yet clearly formulated.

He is in that intermediary plane in which the old law fails to operate and the new law is not of sufficient strength to operate automatically without his manipulation. The disciple, then, must first detach from the old set of rules and regulations. They no longer operate for him. His attempt to apply them results in heartbreaking failure, for he does not know why things seem to go so wrong for him. It is then necessary that he detach completely from his mind as coordinates, and free his attention to seek out the new law, to set up the new coordinate and thereby function successfully in the world, though not of it.

In order to do this, to seek the new law, he must accept first the fact that the law which he is seeking is not yet clearly formulated, that its vibratory frequency is not yet of sufficient strength to have built a concrete form on the concrete plane of mind. One of the service activities of the disciple is that of formulating the new law. He does not look, then, on the concrete plane of mind for he will not find it there. He goes above and beyond the

The Disciple and Economy

vibratory frequency of race-mind consciousness, even in its highest concept, to the abstract plane of ideas where he will sense at first the feeble impulse of the new law as it emanates from the Soul on its own plane of existence. He will feel out that impulse, sense its vibration, tune in his own mental vibration to that of the sensed one, and through the Law of Attraction, bring it into his magnetic field of mind.

Upon entry into his magnetic field of mind, the new law, the new impulse, beats with a steadier, stronger rhythm, and what he has only vaguely sensed in the beginning as an abstract idea begins to take shape in his awareness as an abstraction in concrete form. He is enabled to relate the idea to the world of appearances, and to gradually, through meditation and reflection, set it up within his own consciousness as a new coordinate relating the Soul to form. He sees it as a spiritual law governing matter. He separates himself from both the law and matter and sees himself as a mediator. He begins to understand how he can bring that spiritual law, that impulse, that vibration, to bear upon matter in such a way as to produce a desired result in the world of appearances. In this stage of development the disciple is no longer just a channel, he has become a conscious creator bringing two forces together to produce a desired result in time and space.

As the disciple seeks out the new law, he becomes first aware of the Law of Love. He senses its vibration, which is at first very feeble. Before he can grasp the idea in idea form he feels its influence and through the feeling aspect tunes in his mind to its meaning.

Gradually through the combination of the feeling aspect and the mind he intuits the meaning of this new impact, this new law which is the law governing the 5th kingdom in nature. When he has successfully, via the means of becoming the observer, detached himself from

Chapter 1

manifesting conditions, he is enabled to see this new Law of Love in relation to the world of appearances. It begins to take on form. He puts it into words, into picture form, and finally into action. His first application, then, will be in relation to his relationships with people as he applies the newly formulated Law of Love to every relationship of which he is aware in the world of the personality. This provides the new disciple with experience, unconscious experience at first, in seeking out a law, formulating it, relating it and applying it until finally he is told by his Master, "Go forth and serve. Follow your intuitional guidance, my brother, and initiate your service activity."

He finally arrives at that place in the light where he understands those words to mean seek out the new law, give it form, relate it to the daily life and affairs, and apply it for the betterment of the human family. You may wonder what all of this has to do with timing, but you see, the disciple can no longer function alone in sidereal time, for a part of his consciousness has risen out of and beyond sidereal time, and it is therefore no longer subject to the same laws of time and space as he was when he was just a human. There is a new law, a new set of laws which he must seek out, formulate, relate and apply. This he will do as he directs his intuition out of time and space into the world of the Soul and then brings it to bear upon time and space, functioning free of the limitation of race mind concepts.

Discrimination is the ability of the disciple to relate spirit to matter and thereby produce a needed form.

In the beginning, as the disciple begins to utilize the intuitive faculty of the Soul, he is blinded by its light; he is at a loss as to what he is doing, and its light is so great that he cannot see its direction. Remember, the intuition has always been defined as a faculty of the Soul. It is in one sense, the searchlight of the Soul, and

The Disciple and Economy

it must be directed to focus upon that which is sought, up and out and finally down.

Utilize the intuition, turn that beam of light into the world of meaning and consciously intuit the meat of the lesson projected.

Chapter 2

Right Economy

Economy consists of Energy, Force, and Substance,

or Potential, Activity, and Appearance;

I am going to attempt to project a concept from the Disciple and Economy, one which you will later have the opportunity to study in a more detailed manner, to absorb and embody.

At this time we shall make an approach to it in order to expand the group consciousness from a materialistic concept of economy to what I might call a greater spiritual understanding of it. You have heard it repeated over and over that an economy is an organization of the energy, force, and substance of a One Life into that activity which will manifest the purpose and plan of the One Life. Now, taken from there, an economy is created. It consists first of that which is potential; next, of that which is actual; and next, of the relationship or movement between that which is potential and that which is actual or objective. It is the relationship of these, the movement which produces the constant growth or evolution of the economy of any one life, whether it be an individual, a group, a kingdom in nature, etc. For instance, let us take the disciple within a particular group. The actual economy of that which is in manifestation consists of the energy, force, and substance of his mental energy, his astral force, his etheric substance and those forms into which that energy, force, and substance have been molded. This would mean the instrumentality plus the environment and everything within the environment, including time and space.

This constitutes the disciple's actual or objective economy. What is his potential economy? It is The Plan which overshadows him. It is the energies and the concepts which have gone into the making of that Plan within the Ashramic life and affairs. This is his potential economy. The relationship between these two, the movement between them, results in (when they are properly related) forms, the constant evolution of his economy, producing the ever more perfect form of his manifestation. This produces the evolution of the form itself to correspond to the evolution of the consciousness, both incarnate within that form and overshadowing it.

How does one establish this relationship, this movement between that which is potential and that which is actual? This is where function comes in. Function is the organization of one activity, all activities, and of one's economy to serve a specific purpose. Let us look at this. This is right economy. What does it mean? Does it mean, for instance, that the disciple must focus 24 hours a day upon this one purpose in order to serve his particular function? Yes, it does, in that every activity into which he enters and every form for which he is responsible in the world of affairs must be appropriated by him as a Soul to serve that purpose.

Whatever the function is is unimportant. However, let us say that the disciple's function is that of a teacher. This is his primary service plan. This is the way he relates to the Divine Purpose which has moved him into incarnation. It is his reason for being in form, in other words. Let us say that he works at this function objectively and obviously insofar as all of those who know him are concerned, 3 hours once a week, or 3 hours twice a week, or 3 hours 5 times a week. Nonetheless, all other activities into which he enters are appropriated to serve that function.

For instance, his periods of rest, why does he take them? Not because he is tired, not because he likes to rest, not because this is the thing to do. Everyone does it. But in order to facilitate his function so that his sleep at night, his periods of rest and recreation, his contacts with other people, all forms for which he is responsible in the world of affairs, all activities into which he enters are appropriated. There is meaning behind this term. They are appropriated and put into right use to serve this function. He takes his vacation in order to facilitate his function because balance is needed. The purpose for such vacation is not pleasure; his goal during the vacation itself may be pleasure, in order to facilitate his function.

Once the group – that is, all the active members of the group on a discipleship level – grasps this concept of economy, grasps that area within which they are best fitted to serve at this particular time and place and put such understanding into immediate application, then the problems of the group insofar as economy is concerned will have been aligned with the solution and Divine Adjustment will proceed to work out.

The very important point here is the wielding of energy. If you appropriate a form, whether it is an objective object or whether it is an activity such as that of sleeping – this is an activity into which you enter with very little thought or purpose. Too often it is simply because you are tired or because it is the thing to do. The activity then serves little real purpose – appropriate that activity as the Conscious Soul Incarnate. Reach out with the will and appropriate that activity making it serve your function.

The Disciple and Economy

This appropriation is an initiatory act. You will come into a greater understanding of it as such once you begin to utilize the will in this way, appropriating every activity into which you formerly entered automatically (or for whatever reason) such as the act of eating, of breathing, etc. The human consciousness self-motivation is primarily that of survival. The human sleeps to live, he eats and breathes to live, etc. Added to this, then, are all of the emotional motivations, the desires. He sleeps to dream or to escape, etc. The Soul appropriates the energy, force, and substance of all of these forms, because an activity is a form, and in this way, through this initiatory action, he not only sets into controlled motion the energy, force, and substance of his instrumentality and his environment, but he begins, step by step to master it, to make a new impression upon it, to redeem it.

Chapter 3

New Age

The Economy of the Planetary Life;

Creating Poverty, The New Economy;

Right Relationship with the Devas;

Three Motions of Substance;

The Movement of the First Aspect

into the Second Aspect;

Right Direction of Energy, Force, and Substance;

Manifesting a New Civilization

Master John:

As the new age comes in, the shift or the effect upon the lower kingdoms in nature of this particular shift will not be readily apparent to humanity. However, of course it will be very readily apparent to the Hierarchy. For the economy of the planetary life itself will no longer be in control of human consciousness. All life below that of the human kingdom, and I might add, above that of the human kingdom, will take its proper impetus — its proper evolutionary movement. This will not be readily apparent to Humanity.

Now understand that the economy is always the organization of the energy, force, and substance of the One Life, whether that One Life be an individual life, a

The Disciple and Economy

group life, a national life; whatever it is, its economy is the organization of its energy, force, and substance to manifest via a planned activity its specific purpose and goal.

As you bring an idea into a planned activity on mental levels, as you build an energy potential, then you are aligning your own economy with the Universal source of power. The energy aspect of your own economy is the economy of the One Life. Each must dare to find his own relationship within the One Life, to enter into it, to lend his economy to the One Life and to stand the consequences of this.

Consider, you as the consciousness have a vehicle in which you live, move and have your being in the three worlds of human endeavor. That vehicle also constitutes your economy. It is the energy, force, and substance with which you carry out your purpose and plan.

Accumulating materials in order to have an abundance to work with — this is a very hard lesson for you to have to learn. I understand and my sympathies are very much with you, and yet my Wisdom compels me to say to you — work to materialize the characteristics and the qualities of the Soul so that you can build these into your response mechanism. This comes first.

It is a very good fortune (lamented by the group) of the group that the protection which the group is able to invoke constantly, consistently in its invocation of Divine Purpose and Divine Plan, is such as to very often save you from the very brink of disaster by withholding from manifestation much of that which is ofttimes practically making an appearance.[1] Let us go back. For instance, many times this group is right on the verge of

---

[1] See the transmutation techniques in *The Nature of The Soul*

Chapter 3

manifesting a large sum of money, or this or that, or the other which would be disastrous to it insofar as the growth and development of the spiritual consciousness is concerned.

When you have brought into your consciousness such a comprehension of The Plan and when you have been able to internalize the characteristics and the qualities of the conscious Soul – when you can put the materials you speak of into right use without defeating your own purpose, then it shall be given to you. Nothing can stop it.

It is your very good fortune that the protection you invoke has very often brought stillborn some of your thought-forms into manifestation. This is a very hard lesson. You see it is not money you need to work for, it is not material things that you need to work for, even though this seems to be the problem with which you are presented. It is not really the problem.

If you were working in the world, you would not be in this effort. You would be taking a different path altogether and this would be the furthest thing from your minds. When you are able to internalize the spiritual characteristics and qualities, then the facilities for expressing them naturally follow.

The question was asked, "Is it wrong for the occult student to build definite thought-forms to support his maintenance?" I want to answer your question in several different ways. What do you mean "is it wrong"? Now let us dispense with this connotation entirely. It is neither right nor wrong. There is a Wisdom which has application to that which is the problem. In this group life, what would a healthy economy be? Has anyone been able to arrive at, within his own consciousness, within his own understanding, the concept of what a healthy economy would be insofar as the group life is concerned? I would like to know your thinking.

It would be that every individual within the group would be self-sufficient insofar as his economy was concerned and with enough set aside, enough in reserve, always to be a help or an aid to others. This would be a healthy group economy — where the economy of every individual within the group was healthy. Now what is obstructing that healthy economy? Why is it not manifesting? It is not because you do not build thought-forms for material gain. This is not your answer. This is not why you do not have a healthy economy.

You come into this group life to take this teaching. What were you before you came into the group? Were you manifesting what I call a healthy economy? Some were and some were not. Did you have enough set aside to be able always to respond to those who needed help and did you have the Wisdom to make right use of it?

When you come into the work, you begin to invoke Divine Purpose constantly, every day via meditations and your daily activities. You are trying to bring into manifestation the Divine Plan for humanity. You must include the Divine Plan for yourself or you cannot bring it in for humanity. Immediately, when you think in terms of the Divine Plan, you are focused within the world of material objects. This is the material world, so naturally your problems are going to relate to this in one way or another.

Now if you have not learned how to make the best possible use of that which you have (if the economy which you have already set into motion is not serving in the best possible way for your greatest growth and development) something will happen to that economy, will it not?

You endeavor to resolve these problems. Let us say for

instance that you are having such a difficult time financially that you do not have enough to eat. Is the answer to sit down and build a thought-form for enough food to eat? Is this really your problem? There is something wrong in the consciousness. There is some characteristic, some quality, something within the consciousness that is creating this condition within your outer life and affairs. So to change the condition you must change the state of consciousness that is causing it. You don't change the state of consciousness by sitting down and building a thought-form for enough food to eat, because in this way you are merely resisting conditions. You are trying to deal with effects rather than causes. So what is then the condition in your consciousness that is creating your poverty? Find this out, and it will be different in each individual case, though each individual case will be inter-related with all of the others. Find out what this is and then work in your magical effort to build into the consciousness the characteristics and the qualities which are, in their sum total, mastery of the form nature. Then do you think it will be necessary for you to build a thought-form for enough to eat in order to eat? No, this is wasted motion. When it is time for you to eat, the food will be there and you will eat it, just as the air is there for you to breathe. These things are outer reflections of the inner consciousness itself. If you were in a different position where you were not invoking your own soul growth and development, and you were out here in the world of affairs, very likely you would not (because you are in this particular society and this particular structure) be in quite such a financial situation as you now find yourselves.

You are trying to manifest your own field of service in the body of humanity. In order to serve, it is necessary for you to become soul conscious and as a conscious soul to be able to wield certain characteristics and qualities so that these can have an influence in your life and affairs.

The Disciple and Economy

This does not mean that you do not enter into the mental activity and the astral activity at the same time. This means that you do enter into the mental activity and the astral activity and the physical activity which is indicated by your circumstances and your situation. It does not mean that you do not do those things that are necessary to the maintenance of the life and the body, but they are not the emphasis. They do not receive the constant emphasis. This is the meaning of "Seek ye first the kingdom of God and all these things shall be added unto you." You do not make these things the end, your aim and your goal.

Certainly it is all right to build a thought-form for maintenance for instance. Is it all right for you to go to work and work on the job every day in order to bring home the bacon, shall we say? Is it all right, or is it all wrong? It is simply the activity in which you are focused. There is nothing right or wrong about it. So there is nothing wrong in entering into the corresponding activity on mental levels.

But if you go home and sit in your house and work from now until the time you go out of incarnation building thought-forms, then you will not answer your acute economic situation, because thought-forms simply are not the answer. It doesn't mean that you do not carry out the normal amount of activity on all levels. Certainly you do this. Because it wouldn't do you any good either to go home and sit down in your meditation place and meditate to build in the soul characteristics and qualities 24 hours a day and not enter into activity. You would simply go out of incarnation if you did this.

One has to balance his activity and he has to learn where Wisdom is to put the emphasis at any given time. It must be the consciousness itself that must become illumined. Just to change the thought-form does not create the illumination.

Chapter 3

It is very easy for a consciousness to build a thought-form as a substitution for the thought-form of poverty. He can build a thought-form of wealth. This is done constantly by many, many individuals all over the world.

The thought-forms you should be building in order to change the condition would have nothing to do with wealth as opposed to poverty. You should be entering into the wealth of the Soul, and as you brought that wealth of the Soul into your consciousness, it would reflect outwardly.

How does one get into the consciousness of a group such as this? The concept is one which it doesn't want to accept. It presents me, and I imagine would present the Master M, Master R and any other teacher, with a very great problem because, you see, there is a time for this and there is a time for that. There is a season for attention to this and there is a season for attention to that. And the season, the cycle, comes in the life of the disciple. It follows as does the day the night or the night the day, when he gives attention to his consciousness, and that attention is always given at a time when the property of his consciousness is reflected outwardly in his life and affairs. He may have learned through a process of corrective thinking or creative thinking[2] to build certain thought-forms in place of the old thought-forms which he has continually carried in his response mechanism. He evolves and he grows by this then he enters into another season of trials where it is no longer the pairs of opposites manifesting in the material. They are manifesting in the consciousness, and he is working with the consciousness rather than with the form. He looks then at the manifestation of the outer, a reflection of that which is within. It is there within the inner con-

---

[2] See: *Creative Thinking*, by Lucille Cedercrans

sciousness that he works. It is then that he gives up his devotion to the form or to the material to give his energy, force, and substance to the building of what he would consider to be a thought-form to the spiritual characteristics and qualities. It is to him a sacrifice because he cannot see how the quality of love, for instance, can provide for his family. He does not see the relationship between the quality of love built into the consciousness and his ability to provide for his family. Yet there is a very distinct obvious relationship so close to him he does not see it.

How does the quality of beauty within the consciousness give the ability to create beauty in the environment — to build into it that which is beautiful? It is here where you are as a group. That is why your instruction is to give attention to these apparent intangibles in the consciousness level itself, which do have specific relationship with the outer life and that which is reflected within it.

This does not mean that he has no love, but that what he could have is so much greater than what he does have, what he has internalized, embodied, incorporated, that he is living in consciousness in a poverty of love. He may have more love than his next door neighbor who is manifesting more in the way of material objects. But these are the pairs of opposites in the consciousness rather than in the form. And this is how he grows.

We manifest in outer form that economy (activity) which is entered into by the consciousness on subjective levels, the real environment. Every form in manifestation, while created by the consciousness, is a reflection of the intelligent activity taking place on mental, astral and etheric levels.

If instead of having the consciousness of need, we could have the consciousness of fulfillment, every form mani-

Chapter 3

festing, being a lower octave, is a fulfillment. Get the consciousness in the cave of fulfillment, not anything in particular. You manifest fulfillment before you manifest need. In other words, the sequence is supply and demand, not demand and supply.

The first, of course, to manifest will be those of an economic nature as the energy, force, and substance as the economy changes to Seventh Ray, and incidentally carries a certain amount of Fourth Ray. We are coming into it right now in the less than 50 years. By the turn of this century, the transfers will have to be made.

The new economy will not be based at all upon a numerical system, but rather it will be the outer manifestation of the state of consciousness in an entirely different way from what has been true of the past age. It will not be long before the present economic forms – all of them in the world – will collapse.

You know, I don't have the time schedule for the financial systems of the world to collapse. This is something I am not permitted to know, and I do not know if anyone knows. These things are not timed in the higher regions from which they originate and from which they are impulsed. They are not timed except in cycles. We entered this cycle. This brought the cycle into manifestation for this period. How long this will take to manifest its effects or conclusions, is something we cannot know. However the effects can be seen today very definitely in manifestation.

A question was asked, "Are the group financial problems and the energies the group carries symbolic of the problems that humanity will face and are we getting ahead of time?" You ask a very delicate question. Magic, the group magic, does work in very mysterious ways to manifest The Plan. There is a certain amount of truth in this idea which you picked up (if I may put it that way). But this does not mean that the group should become fatalistic and expect to move into dire poverty. It does mean that the group can expect to find itself, both individually and collectively, in real difficulty insofar as the old economic forms are concerned. But as these problems manifest, they can be solved by the new economic consciousness and the rearrangement of forms to conform to the pattern the new forms will take. This will not make millionaires of any of you, but it will make possible the day-to-day solutions which, if you can accept these solutions, will make for the disciple, at least, an easy transition from the old to the new. In other words, you can, through this application, avoid starvation, etc. In solving these problems, then, you will be in a position to aid humanity when they are faced with a problem of much greater proportion: with the fact that the old economy does not work for them.

As you evolve in economic consciousness, try to rearrange the old forms with which you are forced to deal, so long as you have them, into at least an harmonic of the new forms which are not yet in.

The energies which you carry, The Plan with which you are aligned and are endeavoring to embody, are not concerned with a store for next year. In other words, the whole economy will not work. One thing I would, at this point, like to bring out (and it is probably going to create conflict within the group and within the consciousness and instrumentality, and it should — it is time for you to be concerned with this) is that you will be forced, as the change is more evident, to apply the occult principle of sharing much more definitely, more basically than you do now. Do not misinterpret my meaning. It would be very good now to think about this — to come into an understanding of the application of this principle insofar as economy is concerned. Come into an understanding of the meaning here, because eventually you will be forced to utilize it.

Chapter 3

Much of the prison which man has created was that which he created for the future, which is not a part of the Divine Plan for humanity in its economic aspect at all.

It is the concept of saving which has created the block in circulation of the world's resources and has resulted in a very unhealthy economy. There is no doubt that until you are faced with the absolute necessity to change these forms, you will utilize them. It would be of no use for me to tell you not to. But I do say that they have no place in the new economy.

Of course, the state of consciousness is the demand.

When the shift does come, it will be quite sudden. It will be a forced one. Until that time, the best you can do is to try to grasp some meaning from what I have just been telling you and to apply it. That is regarding the rearrangement of the old forms to reflect the new economic forms.

You know, there is one problem that you share with humanity, all of you, and some of you to a much greater degree even than some of your brothers who do not know as much as you know. All have very powerful astral bodies – very strong, well developed desire natures. All of you experience, consciously or unconsciously (and usually it is both) desire for this, that and the other. This is one of your very real problems because it is a block to the incoming new economy. This tremendous force you have created which attacks you, whether you realize it or not, attracts you to the necessities you have formulated or at least that which you have formulated as necessities. This, then, thwarts the new economy and your vision of that new economy. This tremendous field of force you have created, both as individuals and as a group, and as humanity, will have to be transmuted in some way. You see, if it cannot be transmuted by the Wisdom of the consciousness or the Wisdom which incarnates within the consciousness as you learn more and more, then that Wisdom must precipitate those events which will force transmutation.

This is what humanity faces today in the collapse of the present economic systems throughout the world.

The Divine Plan in its economic aspect is, of course, insofar as the form is concerned, very, very different from that with which any and all of you are familiar. There is, however, as is always true in any transition, a bridging work to be done. Insofar as the present moment is concerned, and the overall group life, certain basic concepts of economy must be grasped. They must be understood in their abstractions and in their ideal application, as far as the new forms are concerned. From this understanding as a basis then, there must be applied within the forms of the present system, bit by bit, to alter, to change, the internal structure of such forms so there is a rebuilding from within to without which acts as a bridging from the one to the other.

I shall use an inadequate term here, but one of the very desirable and hoped for developments to take place within the field of discipleship during the past 20 year period has been this very work – the interior rebuilding of the economic form, this certainly in the field of discipleship. As the old form decays, or as the new economy sheds the old skin, so to speak, there is standing a structure which, while not yet perfect or not yet the ideal form, will point the way. It will lead humanity along the right economic path. This is and has been a most important aspect, a most important part of the Hierarchial effort. Yet it has, up to this point, proved most unsuccessful insofar as outer manifestation is concerned. It has been almost impossible to impress the brain consciousness of the disciple in the field with the necessary concepts, because these concepts are (for the most part) contradictory to the basic concepts upon which the private structures have been erected. Therefore, the disciple in the field who must utilize the present structure must utilize the present economy in order to serve within the world of appearances. He is non-receptive to the new concepts which we have been attempting. Certain Third Ray disciples within the Hierarchy have been working on this almost entirely. It has been almost impossible to lift up the attention of the incarnate consciousness to these concepts. That consciousness is so attracted by and caught up within present forms with its good and its bad, so to speak, with all the problems which it presents, that there is a very low level of receptivity to the new economy. This presents us with a very real problem on an outer level because humanity is today moving into that period wherein changes will occur and in this respect, there has not been a sufficient preparation achieved within the physical plane of affairs to meet the demands of those particular changes. It is for this reason, at this time, that not only this particular group but all groups working under Hierarchial direction are being overshadowed with these concepts. These groups are being urged to move very slowly, at least to move in the right direction so some beginning can be made now to build an inner, an internal economic structure or form which will stand revealed when the old forms are no longer serving an economic function.

It cannot be done on an individual basis actually, because the individual, if he attempts to work alone as an individual, as one within the world of affairs, would construct entirely upon old concepts, etc. It can only be done within groups of this kind, and even then, to a very, very small degree. Yet the very small bit that can be done will be of great aid.

The reason why it is so difficult to present the disciple, individually and collectively, with these basic concepts is that their attention is attracted by and caught up within present forms. The first requisite to even becoming receptive to the Divine Plan in its economic aspect is a complete detachment from all those forms known in the world today as any kind of or part of a solution. I realize this is most difficult. I refer now not to you individually or even to just this particular group. I refer to disciples in the field – the field being humanity in the physical plane of appearances. After you have grasped the new concepts, then you will relate them to present forms. But if you try to arrive at a solution simply through the manipulation of those forms, those economic forms now prevalent, you will not arrive at that solution. The reason is because the new concepts are contradictory to present forms. They are completely contradictory.

Your economy cannot simply cease while you endeavor to arrive at this new understanding, actually at a new state of consciousness. But you can realize that you are doing two things. As you deal, each one of you individually with your economy, and you as a group with your group economy, realize that this is a necessity on the physical plane of affairs in this time and place and that it is not the same as the effort to arrive at an understanding of the Divine Plan in its economic aspect. These are two activities. Endeavor to become receptive to that which overshadows regarding economy, as you endeavor to formulate it. Realize that this is a different activity from taking care of the immediate needs. Once you have arrived at the state of consciousness which is requisite to the new economy, then they can become one activity but not until that time.

The first concept to aid the receptivity to that which overshadows has to do with the relationship between consciousness and deva, or the evolution of consciousness and the evolution of the devic kingdom. Make no mistake. What you are after now is not a new form, not at this moment. It is a new state of consciousness that you are seeking: a state of consciousness which understands the economy of the One Life. From that understanding it will be enabled because it is the nature of that state of consciousness to wield the economy of the One Life in the world of appearance for which you as a disciple are responsible. It is not a new form, or a new series of forms that you are endeavoring to grasp. It is a new state of consciousness – a state of consciousness that understands the economy, the movement, the organization of energy, force, and substance of the One Life.

You will have to realize that what you come up with now is an interim plan. What you are working with now is the best possible use of group economy, utilizing in a new appearance, if possible, or a new way, the forms at the disposal of the group. But above and beyond this, and possibly through it and because of it at the same time, you will be working on a different level altogether.

I do not wish to put this into a time limitation but eventually you will be able to formulate a new plan which does account for both that which overshadows, in the economic sense, and the present form that it bridges in an internal sense.

Certainly humanity is responding to a very unstable condition which is manifesting both subjectively and objectively within the world of affairs at this particular time. This will become increasingly apparent as these cycles proceed.

I am going to bring to your attention at this time a concept which has to do with the direction any disciple or groups of disciples must take if he or they are to arrive at any understanding, if they are to become aligned with the Divine Plan in its economic aspect. If you will remember, I said that it is a new state of consciousness

The Disciple and Economy

that you are seeking. Now I ask you to think what this means. It is a new state of consciousness which includes right relationships with the devic forces or the devic evolution. The state of consciousness of humanity in its present development and in this degree not only does not include right relationships with the devic evolution, but includes no conscious relationship with this evolution. This is the crux of the economic problems. Now I am going to endeavor to present you with one or two or three economic problems, depending upon your receptivity and your ability to grasp and to begin to know that activity of absorbing these concepts which are a part of a particular state of consciousness to which I refer. And of course, this state of consciousness is another degree of Soul consciousness above that which you have thus far grasped, identified with and as such, embodied.

For instance, you have heard it said that money is crystallized Third Ray energy. Well, any form is the crystallization of intelligent activity. Any form, regardless of what it is, is the crystallized Third Aspect. What does this mean to you? I am not referring now to money alone. I brought up money because it has been stated as an occult fact that money is crystallized Third Ray energy. And of course, civilization of the past age in the activity aspect has proceeded along Third Ray lines. But now, make the comparison. Any form is the crystallization of intelligent activity, the crystallization of the devic evolution. The crystallized form is but a reflection, a reflected appearance of what we call the real environment, the mental, astral and etheric environment.

Here we are coming to a most important point. The consciousness is crystallized in that it has identified, it has imprisoned itself, within the crystallized form and become identified with that form. Now there is a differentiation here that I want to be certain that you make. While money is crystallized Third Ray energy, any form is crystallized intelligent activity, not necessarily Third Ray; but the crystallized devic life of the real environment — the reflected appearance of the real environment.

What is consciousness itself? All of you are to one degree or another, sensitive to, aware of a vibratory frequency and the nature of a mental body and its reflection within the physical instrument as a mind, the astral body and its reflection within the physical body as an emotional nature, and to a lesser degree of the etheric and its reflection within the physical body as a brain and a nervous system. But when it comes to consciousness of that which you are, consciousness of being within these three vehicles, and of functioning through them into an appearance in the world of affairs, you seem to have very little sensitivity to yourself, humanity, this planet and this solar system as becoming self-conscious, as evolving consciousness or being.

Even within the confines of the reflected appearance or any one of the vehicles – etheric, astral or mental – it is possible by directing the attention inward to the centers, to become sensitive, aware of one's own being as differentiated from form. The essential difference between the human being and the Conscious Soul Incarnate is that the Conscious Soul Incarnate is conscious of himself as being, as being conscious of that which is consciousness.

Now let us try to grasp a little more clearly and intently what this meaning is. A mental body can depict form. It can depict a concept into any outer form, but it cannot give meaning to that form, it can only depict. Consciousness moving into and through the mental body and the forms which it depicts gives meaning to those forms. The same is true of the astral vehicle, of the etheric and of the reflected appearance. Consciousness moving through that intelligent activity of the form gives it meaning – provides it with that equation.

In the past, it has been impossible to even begin to project to you or to overshadow you with the concept, the 4th dimensional concept of consciousness. Now your receptivity is such that this has come into an overshadowing. Therefore, I am going to make the first effort to project it to you.

Think of consciousness. Because it has been defined as you, and because it is defined as you as a being, you think of it as being stationary at a point. While this is correct in that consciousness is focused, it is only part of the truth. For consciousness moves through that point which is its focus within any frequency of substance. It moves from that point or that center into and throughout that sphere contained within what we call a ringpass-not. It moves, for instance, into and through its own particular vehicles which again, in this relationship, are part of the center, in that they are an instrumentality of the center or the focus. It moves through these out into the real environment into the energy, force, and substance of that real environment, and back in upon itself. And when I speak of environment, I include in that environment its sphere of influence.

This is a difficult concept to grasp when one thinks of this in relationship to the individual and then attempts to relate it to the group life; but it is in this movement of this consciousness from the center to the periphery and then back upon itself that a group life is created. This is the oneness and the basis of the at-one-ment of a group life.

Identity is a result of the individuality which is impressed upon a stream of consciousness. Consciousness moves. Consciousness has been referred to as a stream or a wave. It moves in a wave motion and at certain intervals within that wave, comes into, or creates a focus. The individuality (and this is a secret of initiation that I cannot clarify, or even begin to really explain) which sets the wave or stream of consciousness into motion, impresses itself upon each of these points of focus and there then is identity, as a result of that impression of individuality. All consciousness has its esoteric sound, so to speak, but it is not sound or light. These are effects of consciousness within substance.

The 2nd aspect is that of consciousness.

Try again to grasp the sense of this — become sensitive to this 4th dimensional concept of consciousness. Consciousness is a stream. It is referred to as a stream of consciousness which moves in a wave motion, and which, at certain intervals in the wave, creates a focus. That which caused consciousness in the first place, or set the stream of consciousness into motion, that which is individuality and is monadic, impresses itself upon each of these foci at each of these particular intervals. It is at this point in the wave motion that vehicles are created, identity established and intelligent activity entered upon by consciousness as it moves into another wave motion in another direction from that particular point of focus, so that at each of these intervals there is focused identity, instrumentality, life and affairs, and out from these then, a world of affairs.

That is describing consciousness from monad down to here. But also on each level there is a horizontal movement of consciousness, clear out from the point of focus to its periphery, which includes its sphere of influence, and then back upon itself.

It is the relationship between moving consciousness and the energy, force, and substance through which it moves that builds form or results in the outer activity, the outer appearance, on whatever plane this may be taking place.

The Disciple and Economy

The next concept with which I wish to follow this one is a very simple concept, one that you have heard many times. The focus that is created at a particular interval along the wave, is the heart of being at that particular frequency. Humanity is identified within and as the form, being therefore, despite all so-called scientific theories, facts, etc., not then self-consciousness. It is conscious only within its instrument rather than within that center which is the heart of the life at that particular point, or plane, or frequency of activity. Therefore humanity is the victim of circumstance, the victim, so to speak, of appearance.

The Conscious Soul Incarnate, by a certain degree of initiation, is focused within the heart, the center of his being, and that consciousness which he is within that heart or center is that which he moves through the energy, force, and substance of his real environment – creating by that movement the reflected appearance which is his responsibility to Christ in service to the Divine Plan for humanity. The center you all know is the cave in the center of the head. Whatever your consciousness is within the cave, as it moves out from the cave through the energy, force, and substance of the threefold instrumentality and the real environment, is created in the outer appearance.

The Conscious Soul Incarnate at a certain degree of initiation, utilizes his knowledge and law and in so doing he establishes right relationship with the devic forces. He utilizes his economy to manifest the appearance for which he is responsible, creates his function and returns to the Ashram. This is the only economy with which he is ever concerned.

We speak of energy, force, and substance and we relate these to the mental energy, astral force and etheric substance.

Chapter 3

Let us begin with energy that moves, relatively speaking, in a straight line forward, thereby depicting an idea or concept as a geometrical form, that geometrical form or design, being both an equation and the framework — the essential pattern or design around which the completed form is constructed.

Astral force moves in a spiral motion, building a magnetic field within and around that particular framework.

Substance is energy and force moving into a rotary motion. Remember that energy, force, and substance are three frequencies, or three motions, movements of matter. Substance, defined as being etheric, is energy and force that has moved into a rotary motion. It rotates on its own axis, comes into a rotary motion, a denser frequency, and according to that rotation, the total form (the energy, force, and substance of the total form) achieves what we can only define as a directional movement which is analogous to the movement of nerve impulses through the cerebral nervous system.

There must be a certain degree of understanding of what I shall refer to as "initiate consciousness" in order to exchange concepts regarding this. We speak of energy in controlled motion, but the control is established long before the energy and force move into the rotary motion that we call substance. It is the focused intent that relates with the atom of matter, and in so doing controls his motion, his rotary motion, or that rotary motion which it shall take.

If you can become more familiar, as an analogy, with the cerebral nervous system, you will gain a better understanding of substance itself and how each atom of substance is inter-related in its rotary motion, how each is in communication with the other, and a central directing life which is the focus of intent or will within the etheric or the substantial body. As soon as you can detach from the appearance that imprisons its attention, the appearance will no longer remain a problem. It will be an outer effect of the actual service activity, but nothing more.

The first step to take is to become aware that as the consciousness you are focused within the cave, and to realize that it is the movement of that consciousness, whatsoever is your consciousness, whatsoever you are conscious of being, that you are able to bring into focus within the cave. Whatsoever you are there, so you are within your real environment, so you are within your appearance. The problem of the disciple, and incidentally of the applicant to initiation, is to re-appropriate his imprisoned consciousness from the form, to bring it back into the cave, to gather it together into a focus, arriving thereby at a new state of consciousness, and then move out, being certain this time in that outward movement to continue the movement out and back. When it is actually achieved, the astral body is perfectly quiescent until the movement is brought back again.

This is another secret of the interludes. The higher interlude is that point where the consciousness has been brought back to the center. The lower interlude is that point where it is full in its effect or appearance. Once the appearance is complete, what does an appearance indicate? Completion of the activity within the real environment – then is the time for the movement of the consciousness.

When does a form crystallize? A form actually crystallizes or becomes a prison when the consciousness does not complete the movement back from the lower interlude. When it is full, when the effect is full, the activity is complete in its appearance. Now is the time for the consciousness to withdraw from that appearance or attempt. Then the form can be consciously altered with each new movement of consciousness, from effect to effect to effect.

The moment that you realize the appearance (the activity is full in its appearance), the activity, is completed is when the appearance is manifesting. The moment the consciousness realizes this, here is an interlude. The lower interlude is at that moment when the activity is complete, is full in its appearance. Then that appearance or effect serves its purpose during that interlude and the consciousness moves back to its own center. Whether the appearance in the world will continue at all or not depends upon the equation, the manner in which consciousness equates spirit with matter at this high point, or the high interlude. If the appearance, or this vehicle, is to continue to serve as a vehicle, then, as the consciousness moves on into the appearance, there is an alteration in the appearance to serve the continuation or the continuity of the intent.

The inbreathing and the outbreathing is symbolic. The appearance is used by the consciousness to arrive at reality until such time as reality is manifest. Then the appearance is no longer important. It is a reflection. The real work is carried out within the three frequencies of mind, the astral force and etheric substance. This is always where the real work is done. It is the most difficult concept for consciousness to grasp because the consciousness has been caught up, imprisoned, within the form.

Actually, purpose is formulated after the consciousness has grasped the purpose. It is formulated in the mind after it has been grasped by consciousness. Actually the first formulation of purpose (now when I say first I mean in relationship to incarnation of the Soul) is within the causal sheath, by the Soul within the causal sheath. This the consciousness grasps within itself and formulates within the mental body in his mental envi-

ronment. The meaning is in consciousness. Here is the
problem. Of course this is a common problem of all of
you. When you say "form" you are thinking of the physical appearance. Lift your concept of form, a form aside
from the physical reflection, or the reflected appearance
of it. A form is an activity, an intelligent activity, an
activity of devic lives.

A form is an activity. For instance, the consciousness
grasps a meaning. What is consciousness evolving? It is
evolving consciousness of being. As consciousness
grasps or comes into an awareness, an ever greater
awareness of reality or of that which it is — this is
meaning. And it must give that meaning life. This is its
nature. Life is, or the form is life, intelligent activity.
The outer appearance is simply the reflection of that.
For instance, what is the real form of the mental activity, the astral activity, the etheric activity through
which that consciousness is moving or manifesting itself? The consciousness which is identified as Soul, the
Conscious Soul Incarnate, cognizes this. This is a part
of the consciousness. It is the prototype or the archetype
to which the Soul is receptive and he knows what direction or what form he will have these energies take. If
you look for forms such as you see in the physical plane
of appearance, you will never receive the impress of the
prototype. Detach from form as you know form.

I would like to give you much more regarding form,
because again you are making a very grave mistake
here. The consciousness that is imprisoned within the
instrumentality and identified with it must make, in
terms of form and in order to carry out the magic, must
create a predetermined form. But think again. Any
function of the consciousness to serve its evolution, its
growth and development, all of that consciousness with
which it is related, is its own consciousness, its own self
and all consciousness with which it is related. Whatever
that focus of consciousness, through whatever function,

60

is building or doing, it is building meaning. Now I am trying here to give you a totally new and different concept of form itself. For instance, the Soul ideates and thereby concepts are produced, meaning becomes cognizable. It is this meaning that is the form, the perfect form, and as it is brought into relationship with mental energy, it directs the building of the mental form. The consciousness does not take mental energy, for instance, and draw with it a geometric design, a form, but rather it is the meaning which consciousness impresses upon that mental deva. It is the deva's job to build the form. Whatever meaning the consciousness impresses or moves into the mental deva, the deva takes and constructs the form which conveys it, or depicts it.

The consciousness is not concerned with the geometric design. He only knows that mental energy moves in a straight line. The deva itself takes the meaning and gives it a mental form. His attention is to impress that deva with that meaning, to build the energy potential, to attract with that meaning, devic life which will take the meaning and give it form. This is the activity of the consciousness. He has to hold the meaning here and let the deva do its work. He can call the deva to attention. There are many techniques that are used, but the form that the consciousness is concerned with is the meaning. The deva then takes it and gives it form via his own activity. Thus the consciousness sees a reflection of itself, of his own meaning in form. Consciousness is not form, but through his relationship with that devic life, which is form, he does give form or build form. He sees that which he is in a different light, and by seeing that which he is in a different light, that which he is, is evolved or added unto – increased. By the same token, the devic life, as it receives the meaning which is consciousness, evolves, it is added unto – increased. And so the two evolutions aid one another.

Many disciples and many initiates work magic by constructing specific forms, impressing these specific forms upon mental, astral and etheric frequencies. But this is a higher concept than I am giving you – a much higher concept.

There are no words in the English language which would clarify or explain or convey the concept of mental form. Words would completely detract from it. The consciousness must come to understand as he sees it through the perceptions of the mental body without any interference from his physical brain consciousness. It is fourth dimensional and it is constantly moving. There is no solidity to it and yet it depicts. I do not have available to me proper language or terminology which will do any more than cloud and misrepresent what mental form actually is. It is sound, and it has color. It is constantly moving, having no solidity, and yet it depicts in four dimensions. It can be seen via the perceptions of the mental body, but it cannot be seen below, or pictured below that level. In other words, even seeing it through the perceptions of the mental body, it would be impossible for you in three dimensions to convey or to draw or to in any way communicate what it is. Eventually the consciousness will be able to see the form through the perceptions of the mental body. At present it can only be sensitive to it.

It is no longer geometrical in form when it comes into the etheric substance. It is then the counterpart of the physical but of a much finer quality. The inner form is there but it is not perceptible etherically. It is still mental. The etheric form would be perceptible to the incarnate consciousness because it is a counterpart, a higher counterpart of the physical form.

Here again we have a problem because you think in 3 dimensions and your concepts are limited to the solid form. There is mental energy moving into etheric or astral force and etheric substance, and yet each retains itself – remains.

Consciousness moves into the mental and through the mental it moves into the astral, and through the astral it moves into and through the etheric. It should move from above downward. It impresses the quality of the meaning upon the astral. The meaning, insofar as its purpose is concerned, is impressed upon: the mental in its quality aspect, the astral in its life aspect, and its appearance in the etheric. So there is life, quality and appearance.

The problem is that you do not understand what the finished product is.

There is now, as never before, within this particular effort the opportunity to clarify the problem of economy and to find a solution which will result in the forward movement of group service activity. The problem itself is but an outpicturing of the state of consciousness of the group, which is the lack of integration, both of consciousness and substantial forces, insofar as the overall group life and affairs is concerned. While the problem is very much a group one, it is also a problem of humanity as you more or less realize in your observation of the world of affairs. It is a problem uppermost in the minds of most individuals regardless of evolutionary development.

As most of you realize, clarification on this subject of economy has been overshadowing the overall group for some time. There is overshadowing those concepts which, when given written form, will provide the group with text on the subject of *"The Disciple and Economy"* and yet the state of consciousness of the overall group has not been sufficiently receptive to the solution of this major problem to permit the manifestation of this over-shadowing to be brought down into written form. One thing I would have you realize is that any effort under-

The Disciple and Economy

taken by any disciple, or any small group of disciples functioning within this larger work, is not theirs alone. Their success and their own service activity depends upon the effort being made by the overall group as a whole. The conditions (and this should be very indicative to you), the outer conditions which have made writing this material possible have been economic. Due to lack of what you call "finance", lack of right assemblance of energy, force, and substance, there has been the lack of receptivity which is present within the overall group regarding this particular subject.

Consider first what economy is, and you have heard this before. Economy is the organization of the energy, force, and substance of any organized life into that activity which will manifest its purpose and plan. This applies equally to the individual and to the group. The energy, force, and substance, and you can relate this in many ways of the overall group life, have not been integrated or organized into those activities which will manifest the purpose and plan for which it was created. We find manifesting in the outer life and appearance of the group life a complete imbalance insofar as economy is concerned. We find manifesting lack, particularly in those areas which pertain to planned service activity of the group, which is again, the reflection of the lack of clarity in the consciousness of the group as well as lack of proper direction.

I am going to bring this down, and yet you must realize as I do so that this is a very minor part of your problem, to the subject of money itself which seems to be uppermost in your minds insofar as the problem is concerned. Money is directed – it is not attracted. You may sit and meditate from now until you go out of incarnation in an effort to attract into your sphere of influence – money. You will forever lack in this particular manifestation. Money is crystallized Third Ray energy. It is the solid manifestation or evidence of activity. It must be di-

Chapter 3

rected by the First Aspect. I am going to present you with some concepts, which, if you will take them into meditation, may serve not only to clarify but to correct some of the thinking into which all of you tend to fall into.

First, uppermost in most minds is the concept of lack — "there is not enough money". In endeavoring to solve this particular problem, you are making a wrong approach to it. If you will reconsider there is just so much energy (and we will consider this both potential and activity) within the life and affairs of the human family, since money is crystallized Third Ray energy, and since there is an economy of not only the human but planetary life, there cannot be a lack of this energy either in its energy form or its crystallized form. Think outwardly for a few moments to the economic life and affairs of the human family and then lift the mind just above the world of appearances and consider the directional movement of that energy which is really the economic life of the human family. Lift the mind just above the outer appearance and if you do this sufficiently long in meditation and you are sufficiently trained, you may become intuitively aware of that directional movement of energy within the human family — of the movement of energy, force, and substance of which the outer economic structure is the appearance of manifestation. Now if you will keep your attention here, you will realize that the need is not to bring more money or more of this energy, force, and substance into channels of activity which will manifest the purpose and plan toward which you are aspiring and toward which you aspire to serve.

Do you begin to grasp this concept? There are many, many channels of activity potential which will help to manifest the Divine Plan for humanity once they are opened up, but before there can be a manifestation in the physical plane of appearance of any activity there

The Disciple and Economy

must be that right direction of the energy, force, and substance of the organized life as a whole which will in a sense, create the channel, create the path of least resistance for the manifestation of this activity.

In order to overcome this sense of lack, look once again into this world of energy movement: energy, force, and substance, the energy movement of it. Realize that to create a new directional movement to that energy, force, and substance, that is, to create a new channel, takes nothing away from the whole. Consider this — takes nothing away from it! It cannot be added to or taken away from. It simply revitalizes, activates, brings into activity a new area of that life within which it is moving. In other words, this is added circulation.

When you think in terms of solution to the problem insofar as the group effort is concerned, there must be the realization that there is no such thing as lack. Again, this energy, force, and substance of which money is but the crystallized aspect, cannot be added to or taken away from. It can be redirected into new paths of activity. This again, takes nothing away from the whole, it simply adds to the circulation. So what is necessary here is to redirect the energy, force, and substance of the economic life of humanity into that channel which, above the plane of physical appearance, is the new area within the human family. It is organized or gathered up into the organization of the total life in order to manifest the purpose and plan which not only overshadows humanity but which actually indwells it. This will not be done through attraction. You must redirect. Before you can direct this energy, force, and substance you must come into an understanding of its nature and you must approach it from that perspective which will provide you with a relationship within it. In other words, a polarity must be established here between the First and the Third Aspects.

Chapter 3

Consciousness is attracted. That which you direct sets into motion an activity. It sets substance into motion. This is not attraction. It is the movement of the First Aspect into the Third Aspect which sets up an activity here. Then what is attracted as a result of this is consciousness. Consciousness is attracted to that which overshadows it.

There has been a great deal of misconception, not only within this particular group consciousness but within the consciousness of disciples all over the world regarding this particular subject. Every disciple would like very much (and this is due to past experience, guilt, etc.) to sit down in a nice comfortable place and attract to himself just enough money to carry out those small activities which he contemplates. Few disciples there are who have arrived at that place where they realize the responsibility which must be assumed the moment they enter into any kind of a relationship with the Third Aspect. Here decisive action must be taken — energy must be wielded, force must be directed and substance must be set into motion. This generates chaos and this the disciple has to look at, accept and enter into. Here he is setting into motion that service activity which, as it does generate karmic effects, will bring him back into incarnation over and over and over until through the final perfection of his service he achieves Mastery.

One of the first things that you are going to have to arrive at before you are ever going to be able to solve this problem, is the realization that there is no lack. Your lack of money does not mean that there is not enough money and your continual thinking in these terms of not having enough money is defeating your purpose. It is not that you do not have enough or that there is not enough to go around or that you have no way of earning it (which is another bit of a ridiculous concept). The difficulty is that you have not given it direction! You have not related yourselves within the economic life and affairs of the human family within which you are focused. As disciples, over many incarnations, you have abstracted yourselves away from the world, you considered it beneath you and certainly not worthy of you.

Now you come to the time when you must assume your share of the responsibility for the right direction of that energy, force, and substance which is the economy of the One Life.

Fear is very predominant in connection with money and is based upon guilt, misplaced guilt. Every little desire, which as disciples you share with human beings everywhere, every want, even to the extent of the needs, builds up guilt in the disciple. Guilt builds fear and fear immobilizes the consciousness so that the effort to achieve the necessary First Ray focus is lost. The First Ray focus is necessary and, remember, is available to all of you regardless of the predominant energy of your individual makeup. To enter into the First Ray focus, it is necessary to direct, to wield energy.

This is one of the concepts which is defeating our efforts. This is always the tendency of the disciple, to back away from money, or to ask for it. This again is a wrong notion insofar as money is concerned. Money must be appropriated, just enough to do what you want to do. If you approach your problem from a negative perspective, you will continue in the same way that you have been going. You have a responsibility which perhaps you have not yet realized. To the degree that you are able to identify as the Soul and to the degree that you grasp the Wisdom of the Soul, you are responsible for that manifestation within the life and affairs of the human family. Human consciousness today has been given a new opportunity and you are the carriers of that opportunity. In a sense, you are the custodians and it will take the energy, force, and substance of that economy of the One Life to bring about a manifestation of the Conscious Soul Incarnate within the body of humanity. Think a moment! It has been economy that has produced the evolutionary development of the human family today – built the civilization, built the thought-forms which are manifest within the physical world. Good or bad, right or wrong, these have all served the evolutionary growth and development of the human family to this point.

What will it take to manifest a new civilization, a new growth and development of human consciousness? Again, it will take the economy of the Planetary Life itself which is wielded by the human family. Since only disciples capable of identifying as the Soul can actually build those structures within the human family which are the outer manifestations of the Soul, it is the disciple who must wield the economy to this end. Every disciple is faced with this responsibility – to redirect the economy in such a way as to build those forms which carry, which conduct the consciousness and the energies of the Soul into manifestation.

For those of you who back away from money, you back away from responsibility. Money for your own selves is unimportant. It is not money for yourselves that you need. It is how much of the economy can you put to right use? How much of it can you direct to those channels which will manifest the Divine Plan for humanity? This is what is important, not the maintenance of a roof over your head, although this too is a part of your responsibility. But to build the forms which will manifest The Plan within the world of affairs, this is your responsibility.

You appropriate as much of the economy as you can put to right use and certainly your maintenance is a part of that right use. You are very much caught up in the thought-form which has imprisoned the consciousness of the disciple, particularly during this past age out of which we are moving, that it is wrong to have anything to do with money. This is a result of wrong use in the past, a result of wrong evaluation, wrong understanding. Also because you all have the desire, either buried or very much in your awareness, for what money can give you insofar as pleasures are concerned. These are certainly a part of the motivation of the form nature. Because you are aware of them, either consciously or subconsciously, you are afraid to have anything to do with money for fear of furthering this wrong motivation.

Now what is guilt evidence of? The need for redirection of the energy, force, and substance of your own instrumentality into a new channel. You need to redirect your mental energy, astral force and etheric substance insofar as these old motivations of the form are concerned in a new direction. Make use of whatever wants you might have, whatever ambitions and desires you might have — make use of that force, of that power. Make it serve the Divine Plan. Align it with Divine Purpose. Direct it into activity.

So long as you inhibit these things, you have not the power with which to work. Get out in the world and make the effort you would make if you were serving these form motivations. Align them with Divine Purpose and Divine Motivation and in so doing, transmute them, thus redirecting the energy, force, and substance of your own instrument so that you have the equipment with which to function in the world. You have approximately (and I refer now to the entire group of disciples incarnate upon the Planet today) three incarnations in which to equip yourselves to direct the life and affairs of the human family in such a way as to swing that organized life into right relationship with the One Life of which it is a part. Better you begin now for this task is going to require much from you in the way of trained equipment.

You are working now not just for this present moment. The Plan you serve covers a long period of time and in a sense, you are in the kindergarten in your training and your service. But right direction at this moment, during this kindergarten stage, is more important than at any other time.

I might be able to clarify this. For instance, say you are in meditation and you move into the etheric network of the Planet itself within which the energy movements of money are constantly flowing. You have many of these large streams of energy constantly moving and from the large streams, many small streams, all connected. However, there are places where it stops up and this is part of the wrong circulation of our economy within the body of humanity. This has to be approached by disciples within the field of finance as they come into their service activity, this place between the areas where this energy is not moving. Take, for instance, this particular kind of activity. There is not the movement of the economy into that field of activity in which you are endeavoring to function. You are not related within the economic structure of the body of humanity. You have not plugged into it. By redirection this is what is meant – at this point, then, there must be redirected (now again you do not take away from but merely cut a new path for the flow of this energy) from this point to another point, a movement of that energy through this field of activity which has not been activated. There has to be the movement of the economy of the human family into that field and back again into the economic structure.

A relationship has to be made within the economic structure, both a relationship individually and the major relationship must be that of the group. Another concept that has to be taken in here is the organization of energies, forces and substances of the group itself. So long as there is not this organization, an integrated One Life, again it will be impossible for you to relate as such. Again you will manifest the lack of integration via a lack of crystallized Third Ray energy. There has to be a circulation of the energies, forces and substances and a right direction of these of the overall group life into those activities which will manifest its purpose and plan. You cannot expect to do this in a moment or even a few months. You are going to have to approach this with enthusiasm, but not from an emotional kind of enthusiasm which wears itself out very quickly and easily. But from the identified Soul focus which is directing its own energy, force, and substance toward a specific goal.

If you will join hands, so to speak, all of you wherever you are, so that right circulation of energy, force, and substance can be directed throughout the group so as a group you can enter into a group service activity, then your problem will be solved, and you will be ready to solve new problems.

I would like to go back again to this concept because it has relationship to many things. Once you have mastered this particular technique, and in the degree in which you are able to manifest it or master it, you incarnate as the conscious Soul. This is the ability to align Purpose with activity and to indwell the space between as consciousness. You are endeavoring to come into incarnation. To the degree that you are the Conscious Soul Incarnate, to this degree within the vehicle you are able to establish this polarity, it will be established throughout the totality of your own alignment. Align Purpose with activity and indwell the sphere created by the space between as consciousness. Once you can master this technique, you have mastered embodiment.

The economic problem is a manifestation which comes out from a number of other problems. These are subjective in nature and constitute in their totality the lessons placed before the group and the challenge of growth which faces it. It can be resolved with effort as the group consciousness. Each, as it manifests its own foci, comes into an understanding of the nature of the problem. Each one arrives at an understanding of his contribution to it. He can therefore correct his contribution so it is a contribution to solution rather than problem. You understand that where the focus is brought into manifestation on the physical plane, there is the vehicle through which it is possible for the Hierarchy to function. As long as one polarity is in a center, center energies can be released, but center function cannot proceed. The objectification of the service potential cannot be achieved without center personnel through which to work.

Perhaps it would help you to consider what your physical service activities would be as you take up center function. For then, if you include this in your subjective effort, you will be setting up that manifestation into which you will be working, individually and collectively. We come again to the basic, basic, basic problem of the group which does manifest outwardly in poor and unhealthy economy. That problem has to do with the inability of the members of the group to each one establish his own right function in right relationship to each other. This has been the problem of the group from the beginning; it remains so today. There is still too much of the self in each one, so that he does not consider his function in relationship to other functions. He does not consider more adequately how his function relates with the other functions within the group. If each one is focused only upon his particular function and his particular activity without regard to the functions of the other members of the group, then he is not coordinating his activities properly. He does one of several things in his channeling of group energy. In the circulatory system of the group, if he is functioning in right relationship to everyone else's function, he aids in a right circulation and distribution of group energy and group life. If not, he may, on the one hand, divert some of that circulating energy, force, and substance from the group into wrong channels. Or he may constitute a block in the circulatory system of the group, which does not permit the energies to move freely through the etheric network or web of the group. He may constitute a block, either in the reception of energy or the distribution of energy as it moves into the center and as it moves out from the center. Here are three ways in which he can affect the right circulation of group energy, force, and substance, and therefore effort, if he does not properly relate his function to the function of all other members of the group.

This has been a basic problem since the beginning of the group. Contained within it are certain other factors. Not only must he properly relate his function, but he must understand his function so that he can carry it out. He must know what it is he wants to do, how he is constituted to serve in the center and then put his own will, his attention and his effort into that direction.

Once this problem insofar as circulation of the life of the group is concerned, once this is resolved, the outer economic problems cannot manifest. They cannot be because, remember, it has its causes in the subjective life of the group, not in the outer world in which you live. The outer life may appear to be the cause of the economic problem. It is the way you are relating to the subjective life of the group that causes it to be an economic problem. This you all realize to a greater or lesser degree because this is the teaching you have accepted. This is the teaching to which you have responded. Therefore, you must realize that a problem is not the outer manifestation which it appears to be, but rather it is an inner condition, an inner problem, which has to be worked out within the self. Once it is worked out within the self, in right relationship to all others, then the outer problem disappears, for it has no cause, no basis, no fact in nature.

Chapter 4

Applied Wisdom

The Law of Demand,

Sphere of Influence,

The Cause of Poverty,

Goals – The Rule of the Disciple

In *Letters on Occult Meditation*, by Alice A. Bailey, the Tibetan has stated clearly:

> "It is only as a skilful use is made of the supply for the needs of the worker and the work (I choose these words each one with deliberation) that that supply continues to pour in. The secret is: use, demand, take. Only as the door is unlocked by the law of demand is another and higher door unlocked permitting supply. The law of gravitation holds hid the secret. Think this out."

> Alice A Bailey, Letters on Occult Meditation, Lucis Publishing Co., NY, pp. 204-205

Will you each one take the above into meditation and penetrate its meaning?

As you enter into the new year (esoterically speaking), you are recipient of certain major influences to which you will both learn to be responsive and to wield in your chosen service. This is the year of opportunity for you to become acquainted and familiar with:

The Disciple and Economy

1. The esoteric meaning of the term "influences",

2. The influences streaming forth from your Ashram and hence from your Soul to you, the disciple in the field,

3. The influences streaming forth from you, the actor, to those within your *sphere of influence.*

You have arrived in your training as a group at that point of development which necessitates the translation of energies and forces into influences. The result will be practical knowledge – you will learn to be rightly influenced, and in turn to rightly influence others.

This is no easy task, as most of you have discovered, primarily because the man in the brain sees the realities as little more than intangibles. The higher frequencies – the spiritual energies and forces which are not readily apparent to the five senses – are not as yet something he can "get his teeth into", or "his hands upon". He has to learn how to still, seize, and wield them with the mind, via separate acts which are finally coordinated into a service vehicle. The voice, the eyes, and the hands, all centers of projection, of influence, have to become extensions of the mind which carry the right influences into objectivity.

Consider carefully: what are the high frequency energies reaching you from your Ashram, but influences?

And how do you appropriate them for service except by being rightly influenced by them?

We speak in terms of First, Second and Seventh Ray energies. We call them Divine Purpose, Power, and Will; Divine Love-Wisdom; and Ceremonial Magic or Divine Law and Order. We say these are energy expressions of Divinity, but what do they do? Do they turn on the lights, produce heat or refrigerate your food?

No, they influence human behavior. They stimulate man to action according to that mind which:

1. has been influenced by them, and/or

2. has appropriated and is wielding them according to some plan which he has formulated.

They can then be rightly or wrongly used according to the thought-form which directs them.

The young disciple needs to look about him in his environment to observe the many thought-forms actively directing energies and forces as influences into objectivity through the individual, group or mass reaction to them.

Thus through observation, cataloguing, classifying and analysis he can arrive at a realization of that which is influencing his action, as well as that which influences the action of others.

The whole process of human evolution proceeds from the basic interaction of influences upon and within the human family. The man is influenced by that with which he is aligned, and to which he gives his attention. Each man is a focal point or center of a *sphere of influence;* that sphere is crisscrossed with pulsating lines of force or influence, and is likewise contained within larger spheres of the same nature, the interaction of which produces experience and growth. It is utterly impossible for a human being to live in the world without taking part in that interaction. He is both influenced and influencing.

Your task, then, during the next year, both as a disciple trainee, and as an applicant to initiation, is to become the positive controlling factor within your sphere of influence through which the Soul in the Ashram can serve The Divine Plan for Humanity. I refer now to the control of your own nature and not to the control of others. Be certain that you understand the difference — the control toward which you are working is that which consciously and deliberately selects both the inflowing and outflowing influences. Thus will you determine your own action and influence.

Make your beginnings via your use of Divine Purpose as it is reflected in your goals. If your purpose for action is *always* service to The Divine Plan for Humanity, your consciously formulated goals will be selfless.

Example:

1. A disciple is engaged in a business venture. First, why has he chosen this field? Because it is here that his talents, abilities and capacities have led him. He is best fit and equipped to serve here. Business is *right activity* for this particular disciple.

If his purpose for being in business is to serve The Divine Plan (evolutionary growth, development and *manifestation*) for humanity, his goals will reflect that Purpose in one or more ways:

    a. to express the Spirit of Truth in business via best service, honesty, right economy, etc.,

    b. to produce, manufacture and/or market a useful product which serves human betterment,

    c. to become a right economic influence within his community.

Chapter 4

His goals should have nothing to do with the *amount* of money he can make for himself. If they do, they are but reflections of his personal will and are then indicative of a misdirection and misuse of energy.

Money is simply a by-product of work and service, a medium of exchange, and will naturally manifest as one result of work. It will manifest in that quantity which is representative of the amount and effectiveness of one's work if *allowed* to do so. When the natural circulation of money or wealth is interfered with by unscrupulous minds and undisciplined desires, the economy becomes increasingly diseased and will eventually break down in one way or another. The innocent then suffer. The enlightened ones can only begin from that point where they find themselves, through right influence, to correct the condition within their particular spheres of influence.

Money in any sum need never and should never become a goal toward which one works.

The disciple in business, and indeed any disciple within the world who must deal with money and finances, faces *many* difficult decisions. The economic systems of the world do not adequately or fairly take care of the needs of the people. This is *not* primarily the fault of the leaders, as one would believe, or even of the systems themselves. It is the fault of the selfish interests and desires of the people which have created unfair practices, and which are often *represented* in the leadership. From the smallest selfish and grasping half-intellect to the largest one, we see the same practices initiated and carried out to defeat the good of the systems.

Where then is the cause of poverty to be found, and where must the correction begin? With the individuals, the groups, the communities, and the nations, *in that order*.

The Disciple and Economy

It is not easy to take the stand of fairness, of truth, and of true *service*, in a world where business practices contrary to the good of the many are condoned and justified as necessary. "After all it's just good business" has become the standard rationalization common to all. Somewhere, someone (in a substantial number) must find the courage and the "will to serve" necessary to take that stand.

2. The same truth applies to all disciples in all fields of endeavor, and particularly within his field of relationships. A particular disciple has entered into the following relationships:

He is a son, husband, father, employer, friend and co-disciple. There are those who are in opposition to some of his ideas and practices and who might consider him their enemy.

If his purpose for entering into and maintaining these relationships is primarily that of service to The Divine Plan for humanity, his goals will reflect that purpose in one or more ways.

a. In each case, the goal is brotherhood beyond the general goal of brotherhood – it may be cooperative service, loving understanding and guidance, acceptance, trust, care and sustenance, etc.

His concerns should be: what is he doing for his parents, his wife, his children, his employees, his friends and his co-disciples? What Spiritual aid is he giving to his would-be enemies? His goals should *never* be concerned with what he is getting out of the relationship, but rather what is he giving?

This of course is basic and every disciple should not only know it but he should have put it into practice long

Chapter 4

since. Why then are there so many wrong relationships glaringly evident among the many new groups serving in the world today?

Because the practice of truth requires courage, self-discipline, Love of The Plan, *and self-initiated effort.* Too often the young disciple's goals are either subconscious (he dare not look at them) or they are rationalized. Sometimes they are simply overlooked. Every disciple knows that some day he must and will put the truths to which he aspires, and which he loves in theory, into practice. "Someday", "sometime" or "when I am ready". Why not now?

The rule for the disciple in any activity or relationship is:

> *"Let your goals reflect your purpose to serve The Divine Plan for Humanity."*

It may seem a hard rule. It only seems so. It eliminates the non-essentials from your life of service, and brings into play that *Spirit* of Truth which is so essential to right action, and which frees the economy from the control of ignorance (dark forces) to the Forces of Light as wielded by the group Soul.

The Disciple and Economy

Chapter 5

Hold it in the Light

Accounting for the Opposition,

Protecting the Work

Master John:

What do you do with these plans once you have them?
You talk about them. You put them into mental substance. They become very good thought-forms. They go
into the astral waters, and they take on the power of
manifestation. They become magnetic; they align, to a
degree, the mental form or intent with etheric substance – bring them into a relationship with one another. And then they are usually either stillborn or they
are defeated by the opposition in one way or another.
You do not account for the opposition. You do not use
the Law of Economy to preserve and protect that which
you are endeavoring to bring into manifestation.

There is one sure way of protecting your work, and that
is to put it into the Light where negative forces, any
opposition, cannot reach it.

Why should we subject our plans to the opposition to
destroy? Rather, why not hold it in the Light, keep it in
the Light. Regardless of the frequency level to which it
must descend in order to materialize, it can still be held
in Light where it is safe from any opposition.

If you are holding plans of your own in the Light, you
will also still your own negativity, your own opposition

to these plans. As your plan makes its descent from mental levels to the astral, if it is held within a shaft of Light, and under the Light of its Source, then you will not tend to negate your own efforts with astral negativity.

The same applies as the descent is made into etheric substance. As it moves into action in the physical plane of affairs, as it surely must, then again hold it in the Light. Then opposition of an elemental nature cannot touch it.

And as it materializes and becomes a materialized part of The Divine Plan for humanity, hold it in the Light so that its purpose and goal, the Law which created it, may be fulfilled.

This is the best kind of protection that you could use, the right use of the Law of Economy. When you hold anything – mental, astral, etheric, or the materialized form – in the Light, then you are holding it in its right relationship with its purpose and its goal.

Chapter 6

Money

The Law of Supply and Demand,

The Concept of Money,

The Problem of Relationship

There is evidence of a great deal of crystallization in the state of consciousness in regard to money, both concrete form and abstract concept. There is needed a certain clearing of these old preconceived ideas which have been accepted by the consciousness as reality in regard to money.

I am going to take the next few moments to put you through an exercise primarily for the purpose of clearing the mind so that it is receptive to truth.

Take a coin, preferably a silver dollar and write down every thought that comes to mind, regardless of how silly that thought may be.

Stop for a few moments, contemplate these thoughts, and consider why you are not manifesting adequate supply.

Instruction regarding the Law of Supply and Demand is available when the state of consciousness is such that it can accept that instruction, not until.

How can you attract supply, so long as there is resentment regarding that which you are attempting to attract.

The Disciple and Economy

This is a problem to be eliminated only through meditation. I am going to suggest that you take money as a concept, meditate upon it now, and continue daily for howsoever long it will take to arrive at understanding — to view it from mental levels, discuss it from the attitude of Divine Love and to work with it with detachment.

Remember that within every form there is truth and that the major task of the disciple today is to bring forth that truth which is hidden in form into outer expression.

If you will enter into meditation, please, using the seed thought of "money", seeking illumination regarding its place in The Divine Plan.

Here is something for you to think about. In the first place, it requires not only your time, but your energy, force, and substance to get this teaching. It is absolutely impossible for you to begin to embody the teaching without giving of yourself.

What would each one of you do, individually and as a group, if suddenly you were given, not a lot but enough, money to take care of your living expenses? How would you proceed with your service activity from that point? I am asking what you would do if you didn't have to make your living and you could give your full time to your service activity?

I am going to take this opportunity to make a suggestion; to contemplate, to take into meditation the concept that money is crystallized Third Ray energy. There is a great need within the consciousness for a re-evaluation and clarification of the entire subject of economy as it relates to money. This confusion or lack of clarity is in the overall consciousness. It represents a real obstacle to the manifestation of The Plan as it relates to the

Chapter 6

service activity at this time. Crystallized Third Ray energy—money—is an expectant; a form. It is neither causal, in any sense of the word, nor is it an actual need. If money is seen from the limiting perspective which sees it either as a cause or as a need, the disciple is unable to relate in an economic sense within the body of humanity. Money is a form, and is in fact a distraction that can be used as an instrument. I would suggest that you take this into meditation, and record whatever clarifying impression you receive.

After the consciousness has realized the inner Divine Purpose of money, it can then apply the technique which will make it a center of transmission through which money can pass, receive a positive charge and be transmitted throughout the system. The technique is a First Ray technique. The consciousness is polarized in the mental body and is in that instrument positive to the environment and literally to money. He realizes that he is positive to money, that because he is a positive pole he has created a magnetic field of attraction.

The disciple consciously directs money into those channels which will in Divine Law and Order bring it to him. Do not misunderstand. It is not necessary to define the channels to direct energy into those channels which will bring it to you. It will be of aid if you will remember that this is a First Ray technique entirely, that it is accomplished by a conscious act of the will.

You have a partial realization of the Divine Purpose underlying money. I say partial because your realization is very limited. However, it is a very good beginning. It touches upon the fact that money acts as a medium through which those energies which establish right relationship are channeled. Before the problem of money can be solved by the World Group, the problem of relationship has to be solved in such a way as to manifest right relationship between members of any group.

The Disciple and Economy

You are being trained as a group consciousness in a technique which is of vital importance to the World Group of which you are a part and to the humanity which that group serves. As you realize, with the formation of every group there is the manifestation of specific group problems. These problems are shared by every disciple and every group which functions as a unit within the larger group. There is a way of arriving at a solution of any problem and manifesting that solution in time and space. Once any problem has been successfully solved by a disciple or a group, it is also solved for all disciples and all groups.

You are being trained in a technique which, if properly applied, will solve these problems. You are, therefore, presented with an opportunity for service which is very great. The technique is extremely simple. The obvious problem is observed in its entirety in a completely impersonal manner as a whole. It is analyzed first on the concrete plane of mind. After analysis, it is taken into meditation by the group as a whole. It is held in the light. Its solution is intuited by the group as a whole. That solution is discussed until every member understands and is in agreement. It is then taken into meditation, this time for the purpose of manifestation.

It is not important to arrive at a solution of a problem mentally. It must be given form and thereby prove its worth, its use as an instrument of service to the race. Whether or not you accept the training and apply the technique is your own choice, but in order for you to make that choice I have given you this information.

I shall go further and clarify. I do not mean the statement you would make at this time. I mean the choice you demonstrate daily in your activity. The first prerequisite to any group activity is right relationship. Enter into a discussion from a completely impersonal standpoint and discuss the problem of relationship.

Chapter 6

What constitutes difficulties in relationship? Where does the major difficulty in relationships lie? How can it be eliminated and right relationship be established so other problems can be met and solved by the group?

There is no need for tension. With very little effort any group can expand its understanding into so sure a realization that application is easy. I wish to remind you of something else. Right relationship begins within the individual. I am not referring primarily to a manifestation of wrong relationship between group members. I am referring primarily to the quality of relationship which is manifested daily in all your associations.

One other point. Do not in any way take this instruction as a reprimand, neither take it personally. Please remember to keep your discussion on an impersonal plane, for it will always be the way the problems will be solved.

Seed-thought: "Concept of Right Relationship".

After you have arrived at a solution in the problem of right relationship, work to manifest that solution in time and space.

The Disciple and Economy

Chapter 7

Supply

The True Source of all Supply,
Service and Right Use

You realize that any group must become a service group. Each one of its members will play their part in the manifestation of The Plan as it pertains to the group itself. You have arrived at, let us say, the periphery of awareness insofar as group service is concerned. You have not as yet touched upon the vital issues insofar as service is concerned. Each one has traveled in a direction which is bringing into his consciousness a greater awareness of the possibilities of service and each one contributes to the group consciousness in that manner.

I would like to bring to your attention certain concepts which, if meditated upon, will clarify the confusion which is existent within a group mental body regarding service and supply.

You do not take sufficiently into consideration the true source of all supply. I speak of spiritual understanding, growth, mental stability, emotional stability and physical stability. All of that which comes to you as you have become a service group, comes to you for but one purpose. That is the purpose of service. The realizations which you receive, the realizations which quicken the heart, which bring illumination to the mind, have not been given to you as separated individuals to enjoy, to love. They have been given to you as one who has entered into the service of the Christ. Within your sphere of influence there is a need which is demanding fulfillment. The realization which you have received is the fulfillment of that need. While it is important that you obtain a perfected instrument of service, it is vitally important that you realize that such a thing is impossible until you have brought the perfection you have attained into physical manifestation, and that you share it with others within your environment who are demanding it.

My brothers, you need not seek supply. Supply is ever with us, as free as the air you breath. All that you need do is put that which you have to right use. Just as soon as what you have is put into right use, that which can be of further use can manifest just as quickly as the need is manifest. Whenever you are aware of a lack, it is only because you have blocked your channels by not putting into intelligent activity that which you have already received.

Each member of a group is moving out into definite service. Some are being called in different areas, which means that you will no longer be meeting on the physical plane in the physical bodies to discuss the lesson material together. This does not mean that you are not a group, because you do not truly become an integrated group until each member finds his field of service and moves into it, working consciously with those others who constitute his group.

Chapter 8

Group Consciousness and Structure

New Group Awareness;

The Soul, Mind, Brain Alignment;

The Group Structure;

The Life of the Spiritual Soul;

Karmic Relationship Based on Service Activity

The Soul is group conscious. It is impossible to become a Conscious Soul Incarnate as an individual. The conscious Soul can only incarnate in a group instrumentality. We are building a vehicle for this, so that The Divine Plan can manifest for humanity the growth and development of humanity. When we are ready, we will attract those who are karmically ready. I do not mean that they may not be ready yet, but that we are not.

This is why you have entered into the period of testing. A time will come when (to use one of your common expressions) "the men will be separated from the boys" or as we say "the Souls will stand up to be counted". The group consciousness within the individual will make itself known and that which is not of the group (and remember we are not speaking now of a group of people sitting together in one room, we are speaking of a state of consciousness) will fall away. It will be discarded for it is no longer of service. It no longer has value to the evolutionary plan of the Soul.

That which is of the group will go on. It will continue

into ever greater experiences in consciousness of the group – into ever greater opportunities to be of service to humanity. But that within each man which is not of the group will fall away from it. Where will the man himself be? This will be determined by the degree of group which he is within his own consciousness.

If you are wise and wish to grasp the most from this opportunity, you will approach it with joy, for truly if during this period you cry, you will cry alone. If during this period you give vent to negative emotions, it will be alone within your own vehicle. Therefore, approach the opportunity, grasp it, seize it with joy. Welcome that which comes for this constitutes your right to take initiation. Meet it then and have done with it. Realize that inasmuch as you are group conscious, you are one – not only with myself, but with the Master M, with the Master R, and with the Christ. You partake of that oneness which has always been but of which you have not known.

The group is a state of consciousness which is incarnating in a vehicle. You, in your consciousness and according to the degree of consciousness of group which you have achieved, wield energy, force, and substance – never from the consciousness of a separated being or entity.

The individuality is that which expresses the One Life. How does humanity, which is identified each one as a one, approach this awareness of or consciousness of the One Life? How does it become an individual focus of the One Life? The next step, as you were told, is group consciousness. That group consciousness within an individual identity expresses through it. We see the outer appearance of a one thing, a one person, but what resides within that vehicle or that form upon which you are looking? What lies behind it? What directs and wields the energy, force, and substance? What is it that

Chapter 8

truly looks out from behind the eyes?

When we speak of the group, it is the group within the individual, whether he knows it or not, because consciousness is never what the form would make it appear to be. The form, in any instance, regardless of how high or low the evolutionary development, is only the vehicle for a group consciousness.

Groups which come in and go out of incarnation are composed of a certain state of consciousness. They are brought into incarnation by the group and individual Souls to manifest in the three worlds of human endeavor a certain function to which they are karmically related from the past. They may not have completed a certain phase of their growth in one or more of their past lives, either through lack of understanding, motive, love or right relationship.

Each one incarnates then with a certain aspect of The Plan to carry out, both for the sake of humanity's growth in a certain area and for group growth. As the relationship grows, certain aspects of motive, love and right relationship are adjusted. Divine Love-Wisdom ensues, better understanding is achieved, and karma adjusted.

Sexual attraction is most often the culprit to attract these group entities together, because these lives are attracted in that manner. The karmic adjustments will work out from the sacral center to the love aspect as the energies are lifted in aspiration to the Soul's Plan. Sacral energy is a physical attraction. The love aspect is contacted through aspiration and the energies are lifted to the heart where love of a higher nature than physical takes place. Here, then, begins to function right relationship. Here begins the group's attraction of the group plan through aspiration to the higher source and the working out of that plan on the heart level. Here is the

The Disciple and Economy

Soul's attraction from heart center to heart center plus the alignment with the Soul which creates a magnetic field of expansion and attraction, until all of the Souls are touched by this new group awareness.

The interaction or interplay of the energies in the heart center create healing, expansion of consciousness and interplay between the heart and the head. It begins to have its effect upon mental matter which responds to produce thought-forms for the betterment of humanity. The throat center comes into activity. The polarization continues on to a higher level where the consciousness is now becoming focused within the ajna center. From there, he looks down to the heart with love and manifests intelligent activity through the building of intelligent thought-forms as service. He becomes highly activated with a Soul, mind, and brain alignment plus love, and the art of form building has been achieved. He has become a world worker, turning his attention outward from the few to the many.

During this time the growth of the instrument is taking place. Karma is being adjusted on sacral and emotional levels, turning from the sex drive to a polarization between the sacral and the solar plexus. Emotions are impacted by the various emotional thought-forms and reactions held prisoner within the subconscious. Those thought-forms which do not conform to truth are stirred into cyclic activity and are presented from time to time to the personality consciousness. If the personality is still caught up in the emotions, it can't get out and the cycle goes back into the lower realms until another opportunity presents itself for this particular block to show itself again.

This group consciousness now begins to attract students into its center. They have been hovering on the periphery of the nucleus and have been in contact with certain members of the group.

Chapter 8

When the group has adjusted to a fine quality of transmitted light, it is then ready to begin teaching these Souls which are ready for group instruction.

The students have been looking and reading, searching for they know not what. The contacts made by the group seem like old friends because they are, through past incarnations. They are familiar and therefore trust that the nucleus group will not lead them astray.

There will be karmic adjustments made, easier this time because of the power to good of the group. The expansion of consciousness will come easier than it did for the main group due to the energies of the Soul being attracted to it.

The new students will bring in their associates and there will be rapid expansion of students and group consciousness.

We come now to the individuals within the group seeking help to adjust their karma so they will be able to serve. Each one is aware of certain blocks where they are unable to perform. Each one is aware of inadequacies which, with very little effort, can be transmuted.

Each one feels a certain responsibility to the group to correct these problems so they may be free to serve. The main concern is not for the separated self but to be able to lift the awareness high enough to allow the Soul's light to penetrate this darkness.

This group fights its way to the top and works together in spite of its manifesting conditions. It proceeds as if these limitations were not present – it supersedes them.

As the group's light magnifies in radiatory light, going outward in service, that light cannot help but flow into the subconscious to stimulate these thought-forms and bring them up to the surface where they can be seen and handled by the consciousness. This is where the disciple is asked to proceed on faith, knowing full well that these problems will be absolved by the Soul itself.

When the consciousness can focus within the heart center, it can usually deal with those reactions and can become more detached, free of emotion, and can look at the circumstances. Then the opportunity presents itself where the problem can be solved.

Some deep rooted problems within the astral may have to wait until the Soul, mind, and brain alignment is consummated before they can be adjusted, for it takes the light of the Soul purposely focused into the astral to get at the deep seated problems and transmute them.

The whole time this has been going on in one individual it has been going on in the group of individuals, for growth cannot proceed for only the one. It is group relationship, group reaction, group solving that is working out through this magnetic field. One lifts the other in consciousness until the door is opened for all as a group to proceed through the open door of understanding, wisdom and light.

Through all of this growth, the etheric lines of light have been built in an expanding array of lines of force, binding one another into a state of ever expanding consciousness. Where one has a certain stage of development to work out, another is involved in a particular relationship to work out, etc.

The group is aligned through the astral body (now cleared to a great degree of karmic obligations) and capable of the finest reflection of group purpose and goal, capable of reflecting in the clearest and most precise manner, the thought-forms the group decides to manifest into Divine Activity.

Chapter 8

The mental body of the group has become aligned in purpose and goal with the group soul's Divine Plan and can produce within the group life a positive creative force. It draws on the powers which help humanity formulate its purpose and goal. The group progress thus far has created an unconscious rise in frequency within humanity.

The group has now become a transmitter for higher spiritual force. Because of its combined motive, it maintains the highest degree possible of spiritual energies being precipitated into the body of humanity for its evolutionary growth and development.

The group consciousness is at a very low tonal quality when it comes together for the first time as a study group. Individuals tend to hold back, become self-conscious, feel inadequate or tend to hold onto what they have accepted in the past as truth.

This is true in the beginning, and it takes a great deal of manipulation on the part of the teacher to get people to open up, to lend themselves to the group growth rather than withdrawing into a shell.

Once this first major step has been taken, then the group integration proceeds into a gradual lifting into higher frequencies.

As people turn from themselves to the group structure, it becomes much easier to absorb and transmute differences and a spirit of camaraderie begins to form.

All of this time alignments are being built and the energies are beginning to be felt.

Be very careful to warn the group to avoid becoming too personally involved with another's personality problems. Detachment and brotherhood must be the key to group fulfillment. Love each member as much, no one less or more.

The group magnetic field will now become stronger through the Wisdom trickling in and increasing acceptance as integration takes place and the truth of the Wisdom stands the test of daily activities.

Proceed slowly with lower alignments and center expansion so that it is a group alignment and expansion. Individuals may feel the need to hurry, others to take more time. Take the time to stabilize each phase for the group so that one will not hurry on while another may hold back. The group needs to know that it is helping each member to adjust and expand on a daily basis.

We may meet once a week or however often seems wise, but the important feature of group homework is meeting on a daily basis subjectively and helping one another in morning meditation, at noon with the World Group and at bed time to re-establish alignments with one another and as a Group Soul.

The magnetic field is an important part of group development, both as a healing agent and an important function within the student's environment, as an attractive force to attract karmically related members and to hold the nucleus with the intent of The Divine Plan in service to humanity.

Group expansion is a prerequisite of service. If the teaching cannot be utilized in service every moment, then its function will not expand. Each must hold the key to group survival.

Group expansion will grow through daily meditation, subjective activity and aspiration to the group portion of The Divine Plan and its evolutionary development. This has a direct impact on humanity as a whole state of

Chapter 8

consciousness.

When you meditate and there is "nothing there", remember that it is your aspiration that causes the attention of the Soul to shine forth and bathe you in its energy. It takes discipline at meditating, and it takes time for the cycles to develop.

Remember that you are the initiator. You are creating the magic; you are setting the stage for the great play to begin.

What you are doing through your alignments, aspiration, and meditations is setting into motion Divine forces which move energy, which create vortices and which awaken sleeping centers into activity.

If you think on this, you will see that you are creating a dynamic influence within your threefold body and your surrounding environment.

You are, by your work within the cave, contacting Souls with which you are not even aware, both in your environment and out of incarnation. The cave is your point of contact, but to arrive at that point involves a great deal of preparation.

As stated previously, you have alignments to build, centers to activate, lines of light to repeatedly build and maintain; a constant center of focus within the ajna is essential.

As the mis-used and mis-informed subconscious manifestations rear their ugly heads, they have to be brought up to the attention of the Soul where they can be transmuted into light.

Then there is the creation of a positive and negative force between the Soul and the personality which must

The Disciple and Economy

be held constantly as the Service Plan of the Soul unfolds into conscious personality awareness.

Each emotional or physical upheaval draws the attention back to the threefold vehicle; but handled from the focus of the Soul infused personality, these become few and far between as the personality stabilizes in its service function.

The Soul infused personality serves by becoming an instrument through which the Hierarchy can channel the energies necessary for humanity's next evolutionary step.

The channeling of the instrument brings all of those within the environment into a more stabilized attitude simply because of its stabilizing influence.

It has already run through the gamut of worldly chaos, so it is not easily disturbed by emotions: his own or others. As he lives, breathes and thinks in the light of the Soul, he is influencing all humans, animals, vegetation and minerals by his presence.

So you see, each one of you has a very powerful effect as you live, move and have your being in the three worlds of human endeavor.

Now when you become part of a group consciousness, you not only lift yourself higher through aspiration, alignment and discipline, you also lift your brothers as one, stabilizing them as you meet and discuss Truth.

Now do you begin to glimpse the wonders back of all you see? Think of the Truth being held for humanity by the Great Minds, waiting for someone with stability and one-pointed effort to align with that field of service to aid humanity. Think of the energy, force, and substance that can be tapped at that level for humanity. Think of the power you have when your motives become pure.

The Truth must be brought into incarnation in its purest form to be worthwhile to humanity. There is enough distortion in this world already without adding to it.

A Group consciousness focusing on these truths will be able to grasp the energy and power of these concepts and make an impression upon a waiting humanity.

When one person is depressed within a group, take the time to listen to what they are saying. Where is their focus of attention? It is where they have been all day: working around people, around their kids at home, etc. How does the group lift up these people, how do you get their attention?

First you align one another with love, calming the physical and emotional group body. Then you consciously lift them to the mental body where reason can take command.

Very often the group is despondent due to lack of service function, or the cycle is that of lack of activity spiritually and the need for aspiration or precipitation takes precedence.

These are just as important as a good productive discussion meeting, although students tend to criticize when they are not in tune with the cycle.

The group must realize where the group is functioning so that it does not waiver from the path.

Some cycles produce much discussion, at other times, there is warmth and friendship and still at other times the attention is turned upward in aspiration as the concepts flow into the group magnetic field.

The Disciple and Economy

Learn to portray the sound of the group. Lend yourself to it; then as you become receptive to higher impulse and the magnetic field, begin to lift as a group, to re-establish group vitality, focus, aspiration and longing toward the light.

Some students would drop out or become discouraged because the group was not performing according to their expectations. If they can be convinced that a cycle is manifesting, the group consciousness will be accepted much more easily.

Dare to throw out any preconceived ideas about how the group should function. Come to the meeting open and with love. Share in what the group is feeling at the moment. Discuss its inner workings. Through the various thought-forms that the group is holding will come renewed growth through understanding and receptivity.

We have already arrived at that point where there is the beginning of the realization that each individual is an aggregate of consciousness which actually constitutes a group life. To become group conscious, is it not then reasonable to consider that the first step which must be taken is to be conscious – to become conscious – fully conscious – fully awake – fully alert – to that submerged group which actually is the subjective life of the so-called persona?

This is done through a new use of a very old technique, a technique which you have used many times, but this time with new connotation, with new meaning. As you enter into that meditative state of mind and as you identify as the Soul, how far into the inner meaning of this concept of Soul do you penetrate? How much of that meaning do you reflect upon as you identify as the Soul?

Just what does this identification mean to you as you meditate? It is most interesting, though often discour-

Chapter 8

aging, to observe the Western mind in meditation. "I am the Soul"; usually this particular statement is made with great force, but with little depth, and with hardly any meaning whatsoever.

To meditate upon a seed-thought is to penetrate into the very heart of the meaning of that seed-thought: to absorb, to abstract from that seed-thought its meaning, and to incorporate it within your conscious understanding. Therefore, as you reflect upon such a seed-thought – "I am the Soul" – as you identify as that Soul, from this moment on, several factors should immediately come to mind, and as they come to mind they should bring with them a wealth of meaning.

First, that all consciousness, all consciousness, whether it be that of the mineral kingdom, the plant kingdom, the animal kingdom, the human kingdom or higher kingdoms in nature, or whether it be that of a personality long so-called "dead," all consciousness is Soul-consciousness; all consciousness is actually Soul. Realize, then, that this thing that sits here and preposterously calls itself "I" is an aggregate of many "I's".

Here is a group life, a group Soul, which has identified, which has limited itself within this one little, tiny ring-pass-not and goes by some specific name. This technique of identification will be put to a new use then. As you identify as the Soul, expand the lower sphere of your awareness by including within it the totality of that group life which made possible your appearance in time and space.

I do not mean to identify with the many forms which lie below the threshold of your awareness, but with all the consciousness which is imprisoned within those forms, plus all of the kingdoms in nature which meet within you, which give you presence. Realize, then, that this is the consciousness of the Planetary Logos.

The Disciple and Economy

Your so-called individuality is but an aggregate of a group; it is but a process, a process of the synthesis of the consciousness of the One Life in which you live, move and have your being. After this identification has been attained to, and after you begin to realize what it means to identify as a Soul, then expand the upper half of your sphere to realize that just as you are an aggregate of the group consciousness below the surface of your appearance, or your presence, so are you a group consciousness above that surface; and simply identify then with the One Life.

When you have attained to this Soul-identification, you are then ready to meditate.

Now, carry this one step further. Let us take it from meditation into activity, outward into your daily life and affairs. Do not only realize that you, yourself, are a group and that you are becoming conscious of that group which you are, but that so is every other so-called individual with whom you come in contact a group; that as you relate to that individual, you must do so as a group to a group; that right relationship manifests as brotherhood because the totality of each group is brought into rapport in love, so to speak, with each other.

Before you dare to enter into the field of teaching, this realization, this identification, and finally, this group consciousness, must for you become a reality within your mind. You serve always the many. You serve always, regardless of what focus it might be through, the One Life as it manifests in myriad group forms.

Before we are through with this subject, I am going to discuss fully with you a point which is most important – the mergence of the overshadowing Soul, or that aspect of the consciousness which is actually related to the higher kingdoms in nature, with the indwelling or imprisoned consciousness. For integration means just what the term implies; it is the establishment of integrity, the spiritual integrity of the totality of the group or the Soul.

At this time, however, we shall not go into this mergence, but rather I leave you with this concept to reflect upon, to meditate upon and to begin to embody, to incorporate within your own consciousness and instrument as you express the concept in your daily life and affairs. Ask yourself several questions: "How have you expressed the concept which has been projected in this lesson? How has this concept changed your attitude? How has it expanded your awareness? Has it in any way, and in what way, manifested in your outer life and affairs?"

Remember, this will not only be in relationship to the outer life and contacts, it will be with yourself as well. Do not forget that it is just as necessary for you to establish right relationship within yourself as outside of yourself. All of these various factors must be brought into right relationship and peace established within that group consciousness which you are, before you can possibly begin to manifest right relationship, or brotherhood, outwardly. This you must understand.

And now I am going to just touch upon one other concept which will aid in your future contemplation, in expansion of consciousness, regarding the so-called subconscious. That area of the subconscious which contains the many personas described in the foregoing, plus the many evaluations which have been made, plus the wish-life, is defined as the "area of embodied growth".

MEDITATION

Become physically relaxed and comfortable, emotionally

calm and serene, mentally poised and alert. Focus the consciousness in the ajna center and integrate the total personality via the sounding of the OM.

Upon a line of light, withdraw the focus of consciousness in the ajna center into the cave in the center of the head and identify as the Soul.

Lift that focus of consciousness from the cave into the head center and identify with the One Life by meditating upon the seed-thought "I am the One and the Many".

Now consider the purpose of the One Planetary life which is working out through the body of humanity.

Relax the attention and return to the normal focus.

How does the individual disciple become group conscious? There are many related factors which have to do with this particular growth of the identified consciousness within its ring-pass-not into the ring-pass-not of humanity itself. The first and most important (for it is the basis for the whole process of this growth) is the fact that the disciple consider that he himself is already a group.

The individually identified entity who considers himself to be a human being is actually a composite of many identities which have yet to be integrated into time and space. I ask you to be particularly receptive, as this concept is one which is somewhat difficult to project into the consciousness.

First I would have you consider the very small sphere within which you as an individual are identified. In the not too far past, your identification as an individual extended no further than your own physical instrument. It did not include your emotional nature, nor did it include your mental body, and certainly it did not include the Soul. Furthermore, that small sphere of identified focus did not include within its recognition those entities which had coalesced to produce the physical instrument with which it was identified.

The sum total of the physical instrument itself is an entity which has not been recognized by the conscious identification even though that identification did include the physical instrument. The individual was aware of himself as a body, but he was not aware of the group life which constituted that body.

Every cell, every organ of the body is an entity in itself. These entities plus every atom of intelligence which have coalesced to produce the instrument plus the entity which is the sum total intelligence of the physical instrument, are a group life. This group life has not to this moment, been included in the conscious identification of the individual.

The cell is a composite of intelligent lives. If you will think thus far, you will begin to comprehend that the physical consciousness itself is a group consciousness. I am referring now to the physical instrument itself which constitutes a group life made up of atoms of intelligence (plus the unit of consciousness locked within each atom of intelligence), which has coalesced to produce the body.

Now let us consider the astral or emotional consciousness of the whole entity, that which, until but a short time ago, actually had not been included as a part of the conscious identification of the group. I am referring to each one of you within the group.

This consciousness which is focused within and through the astral body is composed of an aggregate of many identities or actual entities. Let us look at the nature of these many lives. We have, first and foremost, the consciousness which might be called the "prisoner" within each personality thought-form which has masked the Soul throughout its long period of incarnation. You could say, in a sense, that there are many personalities, each thinking of themselves as "I", each dictating actions of the body and of the emotions at different times. This is actually the state of consciousness of the total consciousness until such time as it has been integrated into a focus in time and space.

Let us consider, for instance, what occurs to the thought-form, the mask of the Soul, at the time of the Soul's withdrawal from this particular incarnation. The physical instrument, the physical etheric (and in some cases, or even in the majority of cases), the astral vehicles are disintegrated at the time of discarnation. There is left intact the basic thought-form of the mask, the persona, which holds as prisoner a very small part of the projected consciousness, the personality of that particular incarnation. Here is a form (the basic thought-form of that persona) left, and remaining within it is the basic unit of consciousness that was projected during that particular incarnation. There is locked within it a certain part of the consciousness.

In other words, the whole consciousness is not abstracted at time of discarnation from the personality until such time as that consciousness has evolved to such a degree that it is enabled to detach from the pattern in that particular life which karma dictated. In other words, wherever the consciousness is attached, within that personality, to any relationship, either to an individual or to things or to situations, there that consciousness is imprisoned within that form.

Consider then, the astral body of the individual, which contains the greater majority of these particular forms since the life has, for the most part, been of an emotional nature within itself. Here then, is a group consciousness which is composed of all those personalities with which the Soul has identified, and within which it has imprisoned itself to such a degree that abstraction has not been possible.

You could say that everyone is today, the sum total of all he has been. However, remember that only a little bit of that personality comes into an activity within the present persona (which is what is done in psychoanalysis), arousing something of a personality nature that has been.

This aggregate personality, then, determines the personality of the coming incarnation: the sum total plus the Soul purpose and plan, etc. Consider the present identified consciousness in relation to this group life for which he is the central focus. Always within the present incarnation there is a specific relationship to a particular series of incarnations, or a particular group. Within the personality group, the dominant persona (forceful persona) whose purpose has not been completely fulfilled via or at the time of that particular incarnation, provides the drive for the consciousness or the presently identified focus.

In other words, here is an individual who has not completely fulfilled himself, and it is very obvious in passing to realize that within this particular life are contained the conflicts which give the individual difficulty at various times throughout his present incarnation.

One other point, before we proceed. This group life does not lie down and go to sleep or pass out of existence, discarnate, withdraw, or withhold its influence upon the present identified focus following abstraction from the physical instrument. This group life continues, proceeds with its activity, and the individual is just as bothered out of incarnation as he is in incarnation.

The Disciple and Economy

Now we may look from this dominant, and very influential, group life to another part of the astral consciousness, and we see here the wish life, the sum total of the wish life, which has been created by this aggregate of the many personalities throughout the process of incarnation. The wish life, which again, contains many forms, is another entity and constitutes part of the Dweller on the Threshold. It contains within itself all of that consciousness which has been unable to detach itself from desires, ambitions, wishes, etc. It is very easy to understand why the conscious awareness actually amounts to so little, why the identified focus that does exist within the brain and thinks of itself as "I", is so minute in awareness.

While the astral consciousness contains within itself more entities which are part of the group life, we are going to, for now, pass beyond this particular aspect.

Very little is actually known, either in the world or within the sum total of the group consciousness, in regard to this concept of group consciousness. Therefore, I would suggest before we proceed that you clear your mind of whatever ideas you may have in regard to what constitutes group consciousness.

First, what is it that you will be teaching as you enter into the field of humanity to serve The Divine Plan for humanity? The teaching has been referred to as the Wisdom, and has actually been referred to, by, or in many terms. What, substantially and in truth, is this teaching, this New Thought-form Presentation, this Wisdom, that you will be attempting to transmit into the consciousness of your minds?

This teaching, these concepts, this Wisdom, is the life of the spiritual Soul on its own plane. This is one of the most important concepts for you to take into your own consciousness and absorb and understand. As has been projected to you previously, humanity has entered into a period in its evolutionary development which is of as great importance as that period wherein the individualization took place. The Soul of humanity is attempting to incarnate into its form.

One of the methods by which the Soul shall take up its residence within the brain awareness of each member of humanity is via this teaching, which is actually a transference of the consciousness of the Soul into the consciousness of the persona. Please understand this.

Every concept of truth which you are able to grasp with your mind, to touch upon, to examine, to finally absorb and to understand, is of the Soul. This is but a tiny bit of the consciousness of the Soul. Therefore, each concept of Truth that you are able to take into your consciousness is but the partial incarnation of the Soul into its personality vehicle.

This presumes that you take upon yourselves a very great responsibility. For you become a part of the bridge by which the Soul of humanity shall incarnate into its form.

Open the consciousness now, this minute, and realize that with every concept of Truth which you yourself are able to absorb and understand and later transmit to another individual, which brings him an understanding of this same truth you have transmitted, has been the means by which the Soul, the overshadowing spiritual Soul of humanity, has incarnated into its form.

This, then, is your responsibility as you begin to understand these concepts. This is what you take upon yourselves to do. You become that agent, that path of least resistance through which the Oversoul of humanity shall incarnate into the world persona.

The Disciple and Economy

You become more than a channel. You also embody; you have to be an embodiment. The concepts of Truth as they are taught in the Wisdom teaching itself and in the lesson material are Universal concepts.

Remember our definition of the Soul. The Soul is consciousness. The Overshadowing Spiritual Soul is that consciousness which is identified with and is a functioning part of the One Life.

When you as an individual have received into your personality consciousness a sufficient degree of this Soul consciousness, that is, a sufficient number of truths, and have absorbed that truth to the degree that you have built it into your response mechanism as a part of your response to the outer life and affairs, then illumination pours into the brain awareness and the persona becomes the Conscious Soul Incarnate.

Now, as you take upon yourself, or as you take upon your Soul, the responsibility for the guidance of the spiritual health and wealth of your group, you enter into a relationship which serves to transmit that Overshadowing Spiritual Soul through your own focus of consciousness into the personality consciousness until the group, finally, becomes a Conscious Soul Incarnate.

This is the most important, the most basic concept for you in training to grasp and to understand. For once you understand it, it is possible for you to make that alignment with the Christ which permits your function in this specific service activity. The important concept now is to realize this process of Soul infusion and finally Soul incarnation which takes place in the individual by way of meditation, by way of his own study, and also by way of the group life.

Remember that Soul consciousness is actually consciousness of the One Life. This concept of Soul con-

114

sciousness which seems so difficult to attain, so difficult to understand, is really very simple. For Soul consciousness is consciousness of that which is Universal, of that which is applicable in any situation, in any circumstance, in any event. Soul consciousness is the consciousness of the One Life.

Group consciousness will be the foundational concept from which you will work. This is what we are coming to now.

As the personality, as the brain awareness itself, and the indwelling incarnate consciousness are expanded by the infusion of the spiritual Soul (the consciousness of the One Life) that individual begins to establish on a horizontal level the relationship or relationships which are reflections of the field of relationships within the One Life.

Now, this concept may be somewhat difficult at the onset. Therefore, relax and yet alert the mind in receptivity to it.

In the One Life all factors are known. All aspects, all qualities, attributes, etc., are known and related in a unity of relationship. As this consciousness of the One Life comes down into the brain awareness, the individual in the three worlds establishes his relationships on a horizontal level, which are a reflection of that unity of relationships being made known to him via his vertical alignment with the One Life. This field of horizontal relationships is actually group consciousness.

Now, let us be very, very clear in our understanding of what constitutes group consciousness. It is not limited to a small group of individuals. This is the most important concept and the one which is so little understood by those who are aspiring to attain group consciousness.

The Disciple and Economy

The individual who is group conscious has made his at-one-ment with humanity. He is capable of, and does, establish according to karmic necessity, group relationships with whatever individual or group of individuals to which he is karmically related.

Please consider: most of you have thought of group consciousness as constituting a group of individuals who were somehow related to one another in a relationship which was defined as group consciousness. This concept is limited and somewhat distorted.

Group consciousness is the consciousness attained by the individual who has achieved a realization of the One Life and who is establishing his horizontal relationships according to his realization of that One Life.

Group consciousness then, refers not specifically to the group, but to the individual because he is group conscious. The group, in the term group consciousness, is humanity.

Forget organizations, groups or any grouping of individuals and think only of one group which is humanity. As group consciousness is attained by the individual or group of individuals, this then, will be the consciousness which has been attained, the individual's relationship with the body of humanity as a group consciousness.

Group consciousness cannot be attained via either attention given only to a vertical alignment, or attention given only to a horizontal alignment. It must be the even balance and the equal distribution of the energies via the vertical alignment and the horizontal alignment. This will result in the center of the cross, referred to as the Conscious Soul Incarnate who is within himself group conscious. He is related to humanity as a member of that group.

Chapter 8

It may be of great advantage to you, if you have the time and the opportunity, in addition to whatever other meditation work you are doing, to meditate upon the cross, with a small sphere at the center of that cross, realizing that the vertical line relates spirit to matter, and that the horizontal line relates consciousness to both. The sphere in the center then represents the spiritual Soul incarnate, the Conscious Soul Incarnate, who is group conscious. That sphere then, represents two factors, the overshadowing spiritual Soul and humanity.

You could say that the ultimate in group consciousness would be the ultimate awareness of the greatest number of relationships in the body of humanity. In becoming group conscious, the individual becomes conscious of the relationships within the One Life and then seeks to establish them on earth. In this respect he is externalizing the higher etheric network into the lower etheric network.

Where does this leave us? First, it makes it possible for us to destroy whatever glamour we may have built up around the concept of group consciousness, in that we must realize that group consciousness is not confined to a small group relationship. The individual who has attained group consciousness may or may not be a member in the outer life and affairs of a specific small group unit.

It is very important that the group understands this concept of group consciousness and that they aspire to it, that they conscientiously work toward it and attain it, because it is via this group consciousness that they will be enabled to relate the overshadowing Spiritual Soul to its personality reflection and so transmit that Soul into its form. Therefore, each disciple who is consciously functioning under Hierarchial impulse, is working steadily toward the attainment of group consciousness. In this way he is, then, at the same time that he is becoming group conscious as an individual, establishing a group consciousness within a group within the three worlds of human endeavor, that group consisting of all who work under Hierarchial impulse who are aspiring toward this particular attainment. In so doing, he is establishing a karmic, and I refer to a karmic on a higher turn of the spiral as it relates to service, a karmic relationship with the specific group of individuals within the one group which we call humanity.

You are initiating a new beginning, insofar as karmic relationships are concerned, in that you are establishing a karmic relationship which is based upon your service activity. It is a new relationship within the One Life and while it is also new in quality, it is new in intent and in purpose. Yet, you will find yourselves associated as always with those individuals with whom you have formed relationships throughout the long process of appearances within the three worlds of human endeavor.

This is also precipitating a higher karma, one which relates you more securely and more perfectly to the body of humanity.

You are undergoing growing pains. You will note that I said "undergoing", not undergone, for certainly you have not resolved all of the various problems of group integration and group function which are bound to manifest since they are a part both of the group consciousness and its instrumental forces. However, if as you do proceed with your growth and development as a group, you can realize at the same time that each one of you, individually and collectively, has much to learn, and that each one contributes his share to both the group problems and their solutions, you will be able to proceed with much greater ease and rapidity than would otherwise be possible. You are a group. In order to serve The

Chapter 8

Plan as you have envisioned your service, it is vital that you not only proceed as a group but that you continually grow in group consciousness and its resultant action. In many ways, all of you are as yet separative. The barriers of separation, all of them, must come down. They will do so according to your strength, courage, capacity to place within yourselves and one another those barriers, to examine them, and deliberately put them down or dissolve them. Some of them you have created out of one of the greatest glamours to surround a disciple, or to blind him and hinder his progress, and that has to do with nobility of action or sacrifice, and in this I am not referring to one of you, or two of you, but to all of you. Each in his particular way contributes to this barrier or block insofar as the growth and development of group consciousness is concerned.

Wherever you are separative – whether for what you consider to be a right and noble reason or whether for something which you would not consider so right and noble – wherever these barriers exist, they must, if the goal of group development is to manifest, be dissolved to permit the inter-relationships, the interchange and exchange of energy within the network of relationships. This constitutes group action. It is necessary also that as you proceed, individual functions and group unit functions be recognized, realized and accepted, cooperated with, and that these barriers also come down.

I am going to give you several suggestions as to attitudes of mind and subjective techniques which you can employ as you proceed to resolve your problems, whether they are internal or whether they have to do with your outer service activities.

First, each one is a point of light. These points of light are not all the same intensity, they are not all of the same radiance. Some are greater, some are lesser than the others. But when all of them are blended into one light, the brilliance and the radiance of that one light is the focal point through which the Ashram itself can function in its relationship to the humanity We serve. I would have you remember this, to think very deeply about it, and to endeavor to blend each (his light) with the greater light of the total group. In so doing, see the brilliance and the radiance of that one light and take no concern then with the brilliance and the radiance, greater or lesser, of any individual light. This, while it is very basic, is very vital, and it in itself if it can become the predominant attitude, will establish that integrity, that spiritual integrity, which will make it possible for you to live together, for you to work together, and for you to serve The Divine Plan for humanity together – as One Life. Certainly, each of you in certain degrees, some greater, some lesser (but not one of you fully) understands and appreciates the true meaning of group consciousness and group function. Seek to know and appreciate the fullness of that meaning.

Another point, along the same lines and constituting a technique both subjectively and objectively, when you work subjectively to resolve what you consider to be your individual problems – whether they be in growth and development, whether they are in personality performance, or whether they are in economy, whatever they may be – do not work to resolve those problems alone through your own instrumentality. Can you visualize the group soul, working through the instrumentality of every member of the group according to the activity best suited to the particular instrumentality, best suited to each one, and via that action fulfilling one another's needs, not only spiritually, not only subjectively, but objectively as well? You see, these separations which, for right or wrong reasons, you erect, stand in the way of group progress, they stand in the way of group function, and of group service. During times, particularly now, of crisis, the Hierarchy must look for those group focal points because it knows that no individual incarnate upon the planet today, can alone stand the pressures of the service which will be demanded of those working in cooperation with the Hierarchy. We must work through group focal points. We cannot place the burden of energies, of the tremendous pressures involved, upon any one or two individuals, no matter who they are or where they are. Throughout the world, group focal points working with one or another Ashram, are being trained, instructed and prepared for service in cooperation with the Hierarchy. These groups are our hope for humanity, they are humanity's hope, unrecognized and unrealized. We will use, work through, every one of those groups, every group that can measure up to service requirements, because We need them. There are many, many more statements that I could make to you at this time, many more concepts which have relationship to your growth and development as a group at this time, but I shall not keep you overlong in order to project them to you. I only ask that you take these things into consideration and make every effort, each one within himself, to set aside those barriers which one can recognize within oneself, and to function insofar as is possible at this time, at this stage of your development, as a group, looking forward to a continuity of group growth and development.

I wish to proceed to another subject. This is in regard to your meditation effort. In response to those of you who find it impossible to identify with the persona, I must ask — are you becoming crystallized in a new form? So long as you find it impossible to identify as, or with, or within the persona or any aspect of it, you are still imprisoned within it. Your liberation from it will be through right use of identification, the identification technique. I would have you consider this. Consider again, what is a persona and what are these bodies which constitute the vehicle of that persona? Persona, in the highest sense of the word, and the highest meaning, is the face of the soul, the outer face, the outer ex-

The Disciple and Economy

pression of the soul. To be identified unconsciously as or with anything is to be imprisoned, but liberation proceeds via the use of the technique of conscious identification. Your bodies, the integrated persona, is that part of the One Life. As a part of the One Life, it is a part of you. And while you need not be imprisoned within your misinterpretation or understanding or limitations of it, neither can you escape it. Your evolution will eventually supersede the need for the mediator – the soul – between spirit and matter or monad and persona, but it will not supersede the need of the persona.

The Great Invocation

From the point of Light
within the Mind of God
Let light stream forth into
the minds of men.
Let Light descend on Earth.

From the point of Love
within the Heart of God
Let love stream forth into
the hearts of men.
May Christ return to Earth.

From the centre where the
Will of God is known
Let purpose guide the little
wills of men —
The purpose which the
Masters know and
serve.

From the centre which we
call the race of men
Let the Plan of Love and
Light work out.
And may it seal the door
where evil dwells.

Let Light and Love and
Power restore the Plan
on Earth.

Establishing a Center in a New Area

The Triangle,

An Interplay of Energies,

Working to Manifest Supply,

Make the Need Known

An attempt will be made to establish right relationship between two different areas. Avoid any attempt at guesswork, please, for I can tell you now your conjecture is incorrect. Contacts will be made, if conditions are right, which will lead to the establishment of right relationship between the two areas. However, these contacts have nothing to do with cost. That area is related to this area in a rather peculiar manner and it is important that the flow of energies between the two be brought to the desired vibratory frequency and they be given right direction. Please work in the following manner:

> Consciously link up with the triangle of three individuals in that area without any attempt to know what they are doing or where. Realize an interplay of energies between the two areas via this hookup, then consciously link up with The Divine Plan as it relates to the two areas and channel to the triangle in that area the energies which will precipitate that Plan into manifestation.

There will be a constant downpour of energies through

the triangle, which will be channeled directly to that area. The maintenance of stability during this period will be extremely important for both triangles since the thought, emotional tone and physical activity will color the energy received and transmitted. The other triangle will in turn receive and transmit to your area the energies which will establish the desired relationship. This then, will mean that there will be a constant exchange and interplay of energies between the two areas, an interchange which will initiate a related activity between the two.

The subjective group will carry out one hour of subjective work and the subject for meditation will be "The manifestation of supply as it is demanded by group activity". Do not confine this to money or things, for it is all-inclusive. There should be as little discussion as possible. The meeting will be opened with the Great Invocation.

I suggest that prior to that meeting you meditate using the seed thought of "World Peace". Use individual meditations in the usual manner. If you receive difficulty (reception of too much energy) discontinue them for a time; however do not neglect the subjective activity.

The attempt now is for one-pointed energy. Do not proceed with the ideas you have had in mind. Let your concern be with this instruction.

You no doubt realize that the effort in that area must be supported and backed by subjective activity in this area by a constant inner knowing that The Divine Plan is manifesting in that area. Cooperate with the subjective group there by making a direct alignment in the following manner:

Realize that you stand midway between the Hierarchy and disciples in that area, that you are receiving from the Hierarchy the energies which, when transmitted to the disciples in that area, will manifest The Plan. Work once daily using the form of formal group meditation and throughout the day hold in the back of your mind the realization that the effort is continuous and steady.

They as a group will be working subjectively for the manifestation of supply as it is demanded by group activity. You can be of aid to them by thinking in terms of illumination constantly as you meet the apparent problems in your daily lives. Project this right thought, which is actually corrective thought, into their mental body and thus you will have established an alignment which will carry to and through them into their environment the energies which will result in right use of active intelligence.

You can do much to aid in the establishment of a stabilized effort by carrying forward this activity. Carry it in the back of your minds. Work as a group in unison.

For those of you who are going into a new area to attract a group, you are asked to use the method of evocation for the attraction of finance with which to carry out your service activity, and that you will follow subjective activity with objective activity. You are being asked now, from this time forward, to express the "want" as one has put it, by following the teaching which says, "Ask and you shall receive." When you ask, and I am speaking now of using the spoken word, you are asking the higher consciousness within the personality that you are contacting. You are going to ask for contributions from your audience and from your students, and from any contact in which there is an intuitive recognition of relationship. This is not only a method of procedure which was initiated many incarnations in the past, but it is an unwritten law that you must ask. You must make the need known. This is done not with any imposition of will, it is done actually after sufficient subjective activity, in which the student is left free to respond as he is intuitively guided to do so. I am asking you to use that method.

The spoken word is necessary in bringing the personality into conscious realization of the need. There will be very few students so advanced in telepathy that they will know the need without being told.

Chapter 10

Group Economy

An Apparent Problem of Economy,

Creating A Channel Between Yourselves
and Humanity,

Generate a Creative Economy,

I wish to speak with you regarding several related factors which are of major importance in the working out of the Ashramic plan which you are embodying.

First, regarding what appears as a problem of economy, I would have you consider that you are working with a higher frequency, a finer and more subtle energy, force, and substance than are most groups within the body of humanity, and than is the average humanity as a whole. The energy, force, and substance with which you build your forms, regardless of what kind of forms they may be, is of a higher frequency, a finer and more subtle nature. Therefore, it takes perhaps a little more effort, a little more time, to work it out into objective concrete manifestation.

Among the many possibilities available to a group as it begins to move into the manifestation of The Plan in an area, as it relates to the area, does not mean that things will come to you without effort. It does mean that the group economy which you establish in all of its aspects will be a right economy from which you can enter into your true service to humanity.

The Disciple and Economy

I wish to point up several factors in relationship to this. Along with the many possibilities insofar as a group and its activity is concerned, there are two predominant ones: One, that you could, if the group proceeded in this way, become recipient of a large sum of money with which to begin your effort, you might say from which to proceed; the other, that you could generate within the economy of the group energy, force, and substance, a creative economy which would serve not only the group effort along spiritual lines, but which would serve also to relate the group on a humanity level, if you follow my meaning – creating within the body of humanity a service channel between yourselves as a group and that humanity with whom you are relating – a channel which would also serve as a channel through which the subtle energies of light, love, and power with which you work could also move out, establishing then the right spiritual relationship as well as the right human relationship. This is of extreme importance. As humanity moves through a crisis and finds within the energy, force, and substance of its own instrumentality, that potential which can, when put into right use, resolve its problems of economy, it will be through the right use of work, the right use of business, the right use of what might be called "economic activity".

As you proceed to establish your relationships with the purpose in mind of service, release of your activity. Then you will manifest right activity and at the same time, a right group economy which serves not only the group's needs but which serves to relate the group in its right place and function with and within the body of humanity. In other words, here is the opportunity to establish your place in the world, your place within the body of humanity as a group. Do you follow me? That place can become a valuable place, recognized and known by human beings everywhere if it is one of a true service relationship, that service relationship being not only subjective and esoteric, but being objective and

128

Chapter 10

exoteric, serving the betterment of humanity in all its levels of development. In other words, this is your opportunity to come into the world, to come into incarnation.

I am more pleased with group progress, with the influence you are almost unconsciously wielding, than I would be if you had been handed a large sum of money.

The group state of consciousness potential, service potential, its radiatory influence, all of these factors are crystallizing into a probability the possibility that will be of the greatest service to humanity as a whole, for you to give birth, so to speak, to the Conscious Soul Incarnate within the body of humanity. Relating the Conscious Soul Incarnate to all of your brothers wherever you find them is the highest service you can render, now or at any time. I would have you consider this. You are being looked at, considered, evaluated. Your value, not as personalities or individuals, but that for which you stand, that which you are, is being determined, shall we say, set into motion, for the first time within the body of humanity. That is, you are relating with those as a group who are not necessarily a part of the group. And this is what is important. It is not those whom you attract from out of the body of humanity into the group, but it is your ability to establish your place within the body of humanity. This is the factor of importance. Better to be accepted and loved by humanity than by any person or personage anywhere. Do not be afraid to relate as the Conscious Soul Incarnate, as brothers, within the community where you are placed. This is one of the most difficult lessons for esoteric, occult workers, but it can be learned.

Remember that the energy, force, and substance constituting your economy and out of which are constructed and will be constructing the forms with which you will work, is of a higher frequency, a finer nature, than is

The Disciple and Economy

that which is usually worked with. Therefore, it takes a little more effort, a little more time, more persistence to work out the form, but you can rest assured that once it is worked out it will be a new age form; it will be right.

You realize that the power with which you are working, that which motivates the forms you build and constitutes then the motivating energy, is that of The Plan, the power of The Divine Plan to manifest itself in form. This is your motivating force, the motivating energy. The magnetic force and the quality which goes into your form is that of Divine Love—Wisdom. The true quality and the substance out of which you build your forms is that substance which is derived from the mind of the Christ, the intelligent activity of The Plan itself. This constitutes your economy, your inner, internal economy, out of which you construct the outer forms through which you relate to humanity and through which you serve humanity. How much better for you as a group if you are able to create an economy which serves not only your internal need as a group, but which serves also the needs of the humanity with whom and within whom you are related. Do not forget that there is a reason, an earned reason, earned by the humanity inhabiting the area, for the establishing of any center of a spiritual nature. In other words, they themselves earned the right to that which the establishing of a center in their locale, in their midst, gives them.

It is by being, becoming and being, that that which you have to give will be given, that that service which is your potential will be rendered; not by any outward attempts to convert or change people, but simply by becoming and being that which you have become, within all of your relationships.

One other point I would like to bring out regarding the group economy: if a unit within the group can, whether on a permanent basis or a temporary basis, generate a creative economy as a unit within the larger group for the purpose of serving the internal needs of the group as well as the humanity with whom you are related, it will then be possible for the group to move forward at a much greater speed and with greater facility than if you were to start out now with 3 million dollars. If a group unit can provide this economy, whether these individuals who begin it continue to function in that capacity or not is unimportant, but if it can be done, the group will have overcome its greatest hurdle. For instance, those in the group will complete their training and enter into that function. Establish the function, the office, and then those who can serve within that office at any particular time can do so, and those who are serving within it, and who wish to move from it in order to serve in another office then taking their turn, so to speak, can do so. There are many possibilities and potentials within the group, many of them. You see, while this is much more difficult than being given a large sum of money and proceeding with it, it is of greater value to humanity. For instance, your acceptance will be much greater and of much more value this way than it would have been the other way.

Now I do not mean to indicate that you are cut off from financial support. Do not misunderstand or mistake my meaning, but if you can create, generate a creative economy which serves both the group and the humanity within which the group is placed, you will have taken a major initiation as a group. You will understand the wisdom of this much better at a later date than you do now. Remember, regardless of how apparently good or bad anything looks, you are not working alone.

The Disciple and Economy

Chapter 11

Agenda

Dissatisfaction with Financial Appearances;

Magical Techniques to Bring a Group Life
into a One-pointed Focus;

Economic Value of Thought Life, Feeling Life,
and Brain Activity;

Group Cycle of Activity; Law of Group Progress

First, I am going to speak to you generally regarding your acceptance, your embodiment and your precipitation of the basic concepts of this teaching which are prerequisites to a successful working out of The Plan in any of its various aspects or activities.

There has been from within the overall group membership a constant dissatisfaction with financial appearances in the group life and affairs both individually and collectively. There has been a constant, and I might add a one-pointed expenditure of energy in this direction, a dissatisfaction with results of effort.

If your effort is in the first place rightly motivated, and in the second place if it is based upon a grasp of the comprehension of The Plan, and in the third place, if it is rightly directed, and the results do not live up to that which you have expected or which you have been taught to expect, then it is right for you to question. It is right for you to seek a better way of carrying out your service to humanity. But see to these three factors before you disperse, deflect and divert your energy, force, and substance in this way.

It is impossible for you to achieve any success in your various efforts as long as you are aligned within the intent of the overshadowing Ashramic Plan and the concepts which it teaches, while at the same time you are endeavoring to achieve success via the old methods and the old techniques. This is something you have not fully realized. It is something you must take into consideration if you are going to either prove or disprove the reality or the value of the basic concepts of this teaching and the techniques which it places before you.

In the first place, as long as you accept the concept with the mind and the feeling nature on a conscious level and apply in your objective efforts a different concept, you can expect results from neither, for your energies are being directed into a conflict which negates the outer effect you wish to create in time and space.

It is true that the sum total of power up to this point has been given to the structure, the form structure, already built into the group body itself. The power of manifestation has been up to this point given not to the new techniques, not to the creative magical effort of the Conscious Soul Incarnate, but rather to the tremendous body of forms which have been created in the past and within which you have functioned as personalities and within which you still, to a degree, function as personalities, and yet make the effort to function as the Soul.

There is not yet a clear-cut comprehension of magical techniques sufficient to bring the energy, force, and substance of a group life into a one-pointed focus, giving it a one-pointed directional movement to the group instrumentality and into the group environment, manifesting then that life and affairs which will carry a planned service activity into and throughout the body of humanity.

Chapter 11

It is difficult for you, at this particular point of your development, and while in the process of training, to grasp sufficiently the power of your subjective effort, the power of your thought life, the power of your feeling nature, the power of the brain activity itself, particularly when all of these are combined into a moving, living, manifesting activity.

I hold in focus, overshadowing you as a focal point, the answer to every problem of manifestation which any one of you or any member of a group has. Yet, I find a great difficulty in moving this overshadowing into your consciousness as a group. Endeavor to lift up your sensitivity at this moment and to align it with that which overshadows and consider it an approach to an understanding of the following considerations.

What value, insofar as manifestation is concerned, whether it is controlled consciously or whether it is unconscious, subconscious control, do you place in an economic sense upon your own individual energy, force, and substance? Consider this now. What economic value do you place in a manifesting sense upon your thought life, upon your feeling life, your astral-emotional life, upon the brain activity as it moves energy and force via your physical body into outer manifestation? Consider this first. Do you as an individual endeavoring to function as a Conscious Soul Incarnate and as a disciple within a definite Ashramic endeavor believe that you hold within your consciousness and instrumentality the power of manifestation? Consider it and if you do, to what degree is that power of manifestation utilized consciously in your daily activity in service to The Divine Plan for humanity?

Another question: Are you consciously aware of a group problem in finance or in economy? Are you consciously aware of an individual problem of this kind? What creative effort have you made toward its solution?

The Disciple and Economy

Another question, and be very honest with yourself with these answers for it is in a correct understanding of these that the answer to your problem lies. In your own consideration, within the privacy of your own thoughts, in the tonal quality of your feelings, and in your discussion with other members of the group, how do you feel that this problem will eventually be solved? When you envision a solution, where do you place yourself as a causal factor in the manifestation of that solution? What does Conscious Soul Incarnate mean? Have you considered what would happen if every member of a group were to focus his creative attention for a given period daily upon the wielding of his energy, force, and substance to manifest, first, group service activity, and second, the forms needed to carry out this planned service?

There is within the economy of a group life and affairs a great deal of energy, force, and substance available which can be redirected from its manifestation of individual problems and obstacles to group success into those channels which will manifest in a group service activity. Up to this time, this group has been unable, and this is through no fault of its own (do not misunderstand this instruction as a reprimand, it is not such), to integrate its substantial forces upon any one-pointed direction.

There must be first, for group success, an agreement made between all members of the group, an agreement into which each one will enter, not in part but in total, into which each one will give his energy, force, and substance.

There must be second, after such an agreement has been made or has been entered into by all members of the group, a cycle of activity within which each member of the group contributes his energy, force, and substance to the manifestation in time and space of that which was agreed upon.

And there must be third, the perseverance of the entire group in maintaining that integrated focus, of maintaining the constant movement of energy, force, and substance throughout the cycle. It will then, as it moves along, attract to itself, carry and overcome the sum total of subconscious opposition remaining within the form nature of the group to the manifestation of that which has been planned and entered into by each member.

The first step that every member of the entire group must enter into is an agreement which will create a one-pointed focus of the will energy of the group which directs the energy, force, and substance of that group in a specific direction. I am referring to the overall group life and affairs, to all of those and more specifically to that group nucleus of disciples wherever they are functioning under Hierarchial contacts, those who are endeavoring to work with this advanced Plan.

This may seem to you to be a presentation fraught with great obstacles, yet this is one of the Laws of group progress. No matter what work any one of you individually might set out to do, you are a member of a group, and as such, the energy, force, and substance will be either with your effort or it will be against your effort, or it will be so neutral that it will have little effect one way or another.

When you have a group of disciples, there is, first of all no agreement as to what you are collectively endeavoring to do. In many instances, even though you are functioning as group brothers, and even though on a conscious level there is the aspiration to serve the Ashramic Plan, there is the aspiration to manifest brotherhood, to manifest a group effort. Nevertheless, very often the individual efforts are at cross purposes with one another and not deliberately so, simply because there has not been a coming together, a meeting of minds upon a specific subject, whatever that might be.

The Disciple and Economy

If you could enter into a group experiment which would incorporate into a specific directional movement the energy, force, and substance of the group itself, and you were not successful, then, perhaps, it would be wise for you to look in other directions. Whatever material forms are needed for the manifestation of the group's service activity, are available.

There is no need other than your own growth, and I speak to you now not as individuals, but as a group, for your service to drag due to a lack of funds. It is foolishness. If you are to believe the teaching itself, then you cannot accept this.

The Conscious Soul creates its service activity and it creates whatever forms are necessary to the carrying out to the successful completion of that service.

Just to add to this picture, consider and answer this question. How many hours of subjective effort did you give to The Plan during the past week? Answer this only to yourselves. I do not need to hear your answer. A great effort has been made by a few, but the Law of group progress will not permit the success insofar as the outer life and affairs are concerned of those few. The only way they can be successful, if this condition continues, would be to withdraw from the group and to work together without the oppositional weight, the dispersing of energies, the conflict in purpose and sheer emotional negativity as a result of the problem itself.

I consider that you are now ready as a total group to come to a point of agreement for the sake of an experiment. But in order to do so, each is going to have to put aside his pet objectives in order to integrate the total effort into a specific direction. Certain ones of you within a group, and remember now I am speaking to the whole group, not just to a small group unit, have individual desires, ambitions, aspirations and hopes regarding your particular service activity: what you would like to see accomplished within a certain period of time. This is fine. However, it is necessary for a good many of you to open your minds, to broaden your outlook to a consideration of the group effort rather than just your own, to the group effort rather than the effort being made in any one area, to a solution of this problem on a group scale rather than an individual or a group unit scale.

The length of the cycle is determined by the type, quality and strength of the focus which is first established. For instance, disciples would set into motion a shorter cycle than beginners in an effort of this kind. I would not wish to place a time limit on the cycle, but rather to let you set into motion that which is a natural result of the strength of your focus. What you need to focus your attention upon is that which carries wherever it is, the service potential of the group, into outer manifestation in its particular relationship with the Ashramic Plan and the time and place within which it is focused. What is the effort being made now by the group in service to The Divine Plan for humanity?

The activity of teaching and learning is a part of the service activity. Combined in one, it is the teaching activity that is going on throughout the group, the training activity that is taking place throughout the group, that is the group service at this time. There is that teaching which is being carried out by teachers in the field. This is a service activity of the entire group. These are not service activities of individuals. The teachers who are taking the lesson material into the body of humanity via a group or groups of students are not working as individuals. This is not an individual service. It is their contribution to a group service activity. The same is true of the training that is taking place with individuals. This is a group service activity; it is not an individual one. It is an individual contribution being made by all of those taking part within it to a group service activity.

The group should focus upon the group service activity which is being carried forward at this time and the manifestation of those forms which are necessary to that manifestation.

There is the constant recognition, voicing, and manifestation in a group sense of a problem. That is the lack of funds with which to carry out the group service activity. Students experience this in the effort they are making to pay for classes. Teachers experience this in the effort they are making to teach. In order to bring about a proper balance to manifest those forms which are necessary to the successful manifestation of the group service activity already under way, there must be a meeting of minds. There must be an integrated effort to direct the energy, force, and substance into manifestation of those forms which are needed.

After having entered into an agreement, and remember this agreement should be entered into by all those who are functioning as conscious disciples within the group, then a daily effort should be made on the part of every disciple in order that the group focus is not only established but it is maintained and the movement of energy, force, and substance given direction. It is maintained sufficiently long enough to overcome the opposition of the form to this manifestation.

It would be a group effort, an effort of the entire group of disciples who are consciously functioning within the effort. Therefore, since it concerns the total group, it should be first on the subjective list. If you carry out the subjective effort, the objectification of it cannot help but follow.

Chapter 12

Finance and Money

The Group Soul Comes Into Its Own,

Right Organization of your Energy, Force,
and Substance;

Finance, the Intelligent Activity
of the Physical Plane;

Money, the Third Aspect; Re-identifying Money;

Conducting the Spiritual Kingdom into the Outer
Life and Affairs

I would like to give you some general perspective of the overall activity picture of a group as it is viewed from Hierarchial levels over a somewhat long–range period of time.

With the establishment of a center (and I am including in that statement, the beginnings of the group state of consciousness necessary to such establishment, as well as the formulation of the devic forces involved into the outer appearances of the center) the group soul, in a sense, comes into its own. There is a great need for a certain amount of caution as you proceed into outer activity (and by caution I am not referring to a buildup of fear and a withdrawal from activity as a result of that fear, but rather a caution which has to do with clarity). Make certain as you move into activity (and I am referring now to every activity into which you enter as a group, every activity from the smallest which has to do with the routine of daily living, to the largest which has to do with your group service activity insofar as humanity is concerned), make certain as you move into each activity, and into each step or phase of each activity, that you do so with a clear consciousness; and that from that clear consciousness you clarify your mind regarding all issues which can be seen at any given moment; that you clarify your astral—emotional body in the same way; that you clarify the energies so your energy, force, and substance is moving through those created and opportune channels which are in Divine Law and Order according to your purpose as a group. This is extremely important.

It has been somewhat difficult for a group to achieve a balance between what might be called the objective concrete mind activity, and the more subjective mental activity which has to do with spiritual inspiration. The group proceeds usually (this is the tendency and what you must watch for) with the swing of the pendulum from the subjective inspirational spiritual perspective back to the objective concrete mind logical perspective.

If you proceed into any activity from either extreme, you will meet with unnecessary difficulties and probable failure. Bring these two together. Proceed into any particular activity from or with a technique which utilizes the concrete mind and the analytical, logical method of thinking things through. Then bring down the vision of the soul. Bring all of the light of that wisdom to bear upon that which has been prepared by the concrete mind. Bring in the inspiration then, using the objective according to the spiritual direction, the spiritual perception, the spiritual understanding.

I am deliberately bringing this to your attention before I go into a discussion of finance and money, because it is in this area where the tendency of a group to swing

142

from one extreme to the other is greatest. There are some within the group who tend to function almost entirely in relationship to this particular subject in the concrete analytical mind. There are others in the group who tend to function almost entirely in relationship to this subject in the most subjective area of consciousness and mind possible. These two extremes must be rightly related and they must meet.

As you proceed, you will be presented with many opportunities of various kinds having to do not only with business as such, but with economy on a larger scale. For instance, as I observe a group, both as a center of soul consciousness within the body of humanity and as a center of a particular type, strength and quality of energy within the devic life of humanity, I see moving upward from that center many lines of force. These lines of force are all connecting, so to speak, into and with the economy of the world within which each lives. And I am referring now to the physical plane of appearance. Then the group soul, in a sense, is coming to birth. Some of these lines of force are what might be called good, proper. They are conducive to the productivity of the soul life of the group into the body of humanity via its world of affairs. Some of them are not so conductive or conducive, so to speak. Some of them are potentially dangerous and constitute lines of productivity with oppositional factors. You have not as yet the perspective nor the experience which makes it possible for you to see, at a moment's glance, and to recognize within that moment's glance the desirable (if I may use this term) from the undesirable.

It is very possible that you could be presented with opportunities which would look very good, which would appear to be, in a sense, a pot of gold at the end of the rainbow. Beware of such opportunities. Pots of gold are not come by in this fashion, nor will they be for the group. It is not a pot of gold that you are looking for.

The Disciple and Economy

This is not the reason for your coming together as a group. Your reason for being is service to humanity. Make certain that this is always the conscious and strongest activating force within you. Do not let your enthusiasm blind you to the facts of life in the three worlds of human endeavor, particularly within the world of appearance.

There is, for instance, the possibility of offers which have behind them the purpose of using you as a group to further (and I shall be very blunt, very frank at this point), communistic and even fascist movements within the world. I am not referring at this point to any particular offer which you may have received in the past. I am warning you simply because, as I stated previously, as I look at each center, both in consciousness and in devic life, I see moving from that center, many lines of force which are the lines of connectivity of the group to, with and within the economic structure of humanity. Your energy then, your influence, is moving not in a radiatory field alone as has been true in the past into the world of appearance, but it is moving now through definite lines of force. This type of movement, then, will result in contacts in various departments of human living, various fields of human endeavor; and as a result of those contacts which may appear to happen by chance, various types of opportunities will arise.

Do not then fall for the pot of gold at the end of the rainbow opportunity. Do not fall for anything which does not entail the utmost from you insofar as the right organization of your energy, force, and substance is concerned, insofar as your intelligent activity is concerned, in order to succeed. Anything which appears too easy, give it many second examinations. And in your enthusiasm do not blind yourself to the many forces which are at work within the world. Any group is tested in every new area into which it moves. Your discrimination now will be tested, and you can consider yourselves

144

Chapter 12

to be undergoing such tests until you have successfully utilized one of these lines of force as a channel through which the soul life of the group moves out into the body of humanity, serving humanity.

Do not jump to conclusions, then. When you make statements as to this opportunity or that opportunity, do not make these statements as a result of what you desire to be true, or as a result of your wish life. Look into every opportunity and do not be afraid to discuss it, to consider it, from the perspective which sees its totality as made up of its many parts. In other words, do not be afraid to consider, in this first venture into which you are entering, finance, money. There are factors with which you must learn to work. If you are not capable of looking at the whole picture, you will be incapable of seizing the advantage of whatever opportunity is presented to you. The advantage may not be what it first appears to be.

I am very much in accord with your movement into a physical form which does organize your energy, force, and substance into an intelligent activity. But again I must caution you to proceed with clarity.

Now in regard to money itself, to finance – finance is the term actually which in a sense covers the intelligent activity of the physical plane of affairs. It includes within it that substance and force and that energy which is the intelligent activity of humanity.

This is a most difficult subject to try to clarify to a group whose consciousness is spiritually oriented to a degree, and whose lack of appreciation (if I may use this term) of physical plane intelligent activity is as great as some groups. Your money, whether it be in the form of coins, paper (and I am referring now to money, not to possessions) is your intelligent activity insofar as the physical plane of affairs is concerned. Try to grasp this concept. This is the substance which will build the forms of the new civilization, at least during this period.

Think on this. This is a new concept to you, yet it is an old concept and it is basic. Money as such (now I am not referring to finance as a general term, but I am referring to money itself whether it is in hard cash or coins, actual money) this is your intelligent substance. Your utilization of it is the intelligent activity which builds the form to be indwelt by the spiritual kingdom in nature as that kingdom comes into incarnation. You then look at your money in this light, however much or however little you may have at any particular moment. Look at it in this light. And realize your responsibility in relationship to it is to build the forms into which the spiritual kingdom in nature can incarnate.

Say you have a center to build. The building of it will evolve certainly as your state of consciousness evolves, as your function evolves. What will be the substance that will be molded and shaped into the building of that form? It will be money. This will be the concrete substance that will build this form.

Your utilization of that concrete substance will be your intelligent activity in relationship to or as a part of your intelligent activity, certainly on a physical plane of affairs in relationship to the building of that form.

If you can, see then this money (and do not see it in amounts as you proceed into this) as money that is available to you because you are going to appropriate it as any substance is appropriated. This is where most of you who function in the concrete, analytical mind are going to have to move forward to meet in the middle with those who function entirely in the subjective. The two must come together. You are going to appropriate this money as the Third Aspect, aligning it with your purpose, establishing it as a negative polarity, which, in

146

Chapter 12

relationship to the purpose, and in relationship to your consciousness as a group, builds the forms which you formulate within the group mind.

I want you to understand. The technique should be obvious once you understand the theory. You should be able to see the technique and move into it naturally.

If you can, look upon the money in the world, for instance, as one of intelligent substance, see it as the Third Aspect insofar as the physical plane of affairs is concerned. This is the substance that builds the form of the civilization. This substance is available. It can be appropriated, but it can only be appropriated, particularly insofar as you are concerned, by purpose. See for instance, your dollars and your cents not as dollars and cents, for it is this which limits you in your appropriation of this intelligent substance. You limit your appropriation to your figures, and this again is where it is going to be difficult for you because you would be far better off if you did not know from moment to moment what amount, insofar as figures are concerned, of money that you had. This limits you, you see it as so many dollars and so many cents. See it as intelligent substance.

This is the first step which you have to make in not only the establishment of control of your environment in the physical plane of affairs, but also in the appropriation of this substance.

This is proceeding not from knowledge, but from a faith that is just under knowledge.

The first step to take is to learn to re-identify money. See it as intelligent substance, the substance, the basic material, this physical material (you know all about mental, astral and etheric energy, force, and substance). Let us come down and look at money in the physical

147

plane of affairs as the intelligent aspect which is fluidic, which is not limited in form to amounts, figures, and so on. That substance, which, according to your wielding of it, your shaping and molding of it, builds forms. According to your direction, it builds forms.

Simply re-identify this devic life, see it for what it is. For instance, the soul, in order to come into incarnation, must attract to itself the energy, force, and substance out of which it can build a vehicle of appearance.

All right now, the same thing applies in the physical plane of affairs. But in order to work in the world of appearance, the same thing is true. The substance has to be attracted, appropriated and molded into whatever form is going to be used by the soul.

You have heard it said many times that money is crystallized Third Ray energy. You don't have then ten dollars. You don't have ten anything. You have intelligent substance, Third Ray energy, the Third Aspect in the physical plane of affairs, with which to build.

First the soul must re-identify money. This is the first requirement. This takes away all of the connotations which, when utilized by the dark forces, makes possible the wrong direction of this substance into oppositional activity, oppositional forms. When the soul re-identifies it, then he is able to protect it, so to speak, from not only the influence of the opposition, but also from the unconscious, subjective influence of the ignorant masses. This is the first step in the appropriation of substance by the soul, appropriating it as the negative polarity for his purpose, appropriating it as the building material.

This material is intelligent substance and it does respond to the impress which is made upon it. You are not yet at a state of consciousness where you are ready to begin to work actually to impress, except as you re-identify. You are impressing this substance with its true nature.

This is important. As you re-identify money, all money, you are impressing it with its own nature, which is that of the Third Aspect. This is its nature. This then is all that I am asking you to do at this time. I will not go further into technique, other concepts, which are very much related and just as important, because it is necessary for you first to grasp this understanding, to embody it. This is why it is necessary for you to use the term first in your own relationships, in your own world of affairs. Try to employ a new term. In your thought life, think of it as intelligent substance rather than as money. Realize that intelligent substance responds not only to thought and to feeling, but to sound.

Speak of it among yourselves then as intelligent substance, the form building substance within the world of affairs, in this manner: re-identifying it, re-relating with it, and re-impressing it with its own nature. Do not think of it in terms of amounts.

Your progress will be made in your outer manifestations, your experiences which you undergo. When and as you are ready for further clarification, you will receive it. That will be when and as you embody what has been given. You practice, applying what has been given, so your state of consciousness becomes more enlightened regarding this subject and therefore more receptive.

Remember what I am asking you to do, not so much to go inside the form of money and see the intelligent substance within it, which is only energy, force, and substance (again with which you are quite familiar), but to see each unit of money as a unit of intelligent substance itself, in the physical plane of affairs.

The Disciple and Economy

There is not really much love of money, this particular intelligent substance.

The major equation is that of spirit, matter, and consciousness. Once you learn the magic as it relates to this intelligent substance, you will understand why money is no problem to the Hierarchy or to the initiate, because intelligent substance, do not forget, responds to impression, responds to thought, to feeling and to sound. Sound, specifically to sound. This is the first utilization of sound in relationship to it, but it moves where sound directs it. It follows the path created by sound in its movement into form.

You may align if you wish, if you are intuitively guided to do so. Establish your own relationship with it in that re-identification process via the sounding of the OM, so long as you are sounding the OM in relationship to intelligent substance.

I would certainly indicate that there is far too much desire within the astral body of most groups, (if I may put it in very crude terms) to make money. This can become the motivating force. Do not let it become this. Do not think in terms of profit. Think in terms of building those new forms which will conduct the spiritual kingdom into its outer life and affairs, that which will bring it into incarnation.

You realize certainly that tests come in three major divisions, and that the possibility of greed is as great for you as it is for any group. Do not let the making of money become the reason for your activities. This is not your motivating force. Intelligent substance is the negative polarity, the building material, it is not purpose.

I would like to put it in this way. Would you still do it if you were not going to make a profit, insofar as monetary profit is concerned?

150

Chapter 12

You have a good heart. Your enthusiasm is easily stimulated, almost beyond reason. This has been shown in so many of your past experiences. Now, while this good heart is necessary, and while love should spring from it as from a fountain head, that love should not be dependent upon the state of consciousness of the individual being contacted by the heart, or group of individuals; it is clear observation of motivation and the direction in which the energy, force, and substance is moving. In other words, discrimination must be applied and the love poured forth from the heart regardless of what the discrimination indicates. It is a lesson which each group is learning, not one which it has learned, but which it is learning.

Remember I said the first step in the appropriation was re-identification, because you appropriate. At first, the soul must appropriate according to its purpose that intelligent substance which has previously been within the jurisdiction of the persona. The soul, for instance, must appropriate substance which the personality may have in the bank. This is sometimes quite a task. This is the first appropriation. At this point go no further.

It means that previously this substance, this money, has belonged to the persona and the persona has used it, sometimes under soul direction, sometimes under a will-desire focus.

Do not forget that the consciousness which is aware of itself as soul, while it is functioning through an individual focus, is group conscious.

When the world's money, or substance, this aspect of intelligent activity, has been lifted into its right place and function, it will constitute the hem of the garment of the Angel of the Presence. Its form then, or forms, will have changed.

The Disciple and Economy

Chapter 13

Intelligent Activity

Lack of Intelligent Activity,
Materializing The Divine Plan

Master John:

You have been given so much instruction, that you have not seen the forest for the trees, so to speak, nor the trees, shall I say, for the forest. Actually so little of what has been given has been applied, worked out in the daily life and affairs of the group via that network of relationships which constitutes the group and its particular field of activity, that, what can I say to you? You have received instructions, you have received simple instructions, and you have them in the lesson material which has been given, not only to this group, but to any who are attracted to it. The difficulty is in bringing the concepts of the Wisdom, which you have grasped in one area of your mind, down into their applied techniques or science within your very bodies, within your energy, force, and substance, and particularly in your deeds. And so there is a gap between you as the Conscious Soul focused in the cave, aware of the Wisdom in certain areas, and you in your personality life and affairs. A very great gap you are going to have to bridge.

This would come under intelligent activity. You wonder what is the matter with your economy. Well, it is the lack of intelligent activity.

I have words for all of you, for each and every one of you

according to your own light and your own relationship with them, but not exclusively for any specific unit within the overall group. There is much that is important which all of you overlook. This whole area which you overlook is contained within the one concept, one subject, one aspect, and that is in the area of intelligent activity. Your lack of insight into this is almost phenomenal.

The problem I am concerned with is in the area of growth and development. There are two perspectives here. The Master R looks at it from one perspective and He is of course, right. He is looking at it from the perspective which sees you as souls in the Ashram. I have no argument with this perspective. Perhaps because my own position is far below His own, and because my responsibilities are not so great, my relationship with you is somewhat different. It is from a different level altogether, and I prefer to look at your problem from the perspective which sees you as incarnating souls, not so much from the perspective of you as souls in the Ashram, but as incarnating focuses of consciousness within your own brain. It is attempting, endeavoring, making every effort to become soul identified, to become soul focused, to become soul active, and it is with this, from this perspective, that I view you. I would say very frankly and very honestly that you should consider anything you receive from me in this light. If and when it appears that I may be projecting to you ideas and concepts which seem to conflict with those which you have received previously, and which you would be receiving now from the Master R, then realize the perspective from which I do view you and am making my approach. Then to make your choice as to what, how and when, what you shall accept and you shall apply. You realize that you are never seen in quite the same light by two or more different viewers, regardless of the level of development of those who are viewing you. I hesitate in some ways to speak to you. I do not wish to appear to conflict with instructions which you have been given. I realize that it is necessary for you to work from above downward. I realize that it is also necessary for you to contemplate, to endeavor to understand in your consciousness, the higher concepts. But I realize also that there is much bridging work to be done by you before you are going to bring down from the higher levels into and through your instrumentalities, some of the truth (and they are truths) which you look to and which certainly are playing their part in the growth and development of your souls in the Ashram.

The Master R, realizing this must have had some agreement regarding it or he would not have turned you over to me. It is in the area of specific details and activities which you are not realistic. You are together at a certain level of consciousness where you can agree on certain concepts as being truth, but you are not in agreement as to how these truths are worked out, or can be brought into objective manifestation. In other words, in Ashramic levels and within the higher regions of your mentalities, there is an agreement as to various concepts of truth to which you all subscribe, but there is disagreement below this level as to what this particular truth means in this particular instance.

Therefore, a one-pointed effort of the group in any direction has been utterly impossible. This is where I see your greatest obstacle, your greatest problem as a group.

It is not even so much the fact that you disagree in these various areas, but that regardless of discussion, agreements are not reached in certain areas. Even when there appears to be agreement, it is only an appearance. You see, in order to apply the higher concepts and make them work, all those who are within the group (that is all who agree to be a part of the group and a part of its integration) have to work together in a one-pointed focus in order to materialize any aspect of The Divine Plan for humanity. That is to materialize in a process, in a sequence of order, and to have to work so that you can see it. Here it is in manifestation; there is no question about it.

What happens here is that the principle (more often the concepts even above the principles) is sometimes accepted and agreed upon, but there is never a complete agreement within that which considers itself to be a group as to the working out of that principle, its application. When one, two, three, four, five or whatever the number might be attempt to work out a particular concept or a principle into physical plane manifestation, using their vital life energy to do so, several things happen.

Either (and I should not say either, because they happen simultaneously) some members of the group are not in agreement with this and they withdraw from it or they do not leave it alone. They direct negativity toward it. They do not mean to, not realizing the destructive effect of their focused energy, force, and substance, but nonetheless this happens.

Then others agree to go ahead with it, but they do not take any definite part in it. There is no defined interrelated intelligent activity or effort being made. This one does not know what that one is doing, what he is going to do, what is the goal at which he is trying to arrive, and how it relates with the activity that every other individual is moving into. You scatter your energies. You defeat every effort which you move into to materialize anything, good, bad or indifferent, because you cannot come into an agreement. If even two of you could achieve an agreement and then divorce yourselves from the rest of the group and work together to manifest this, you have had enough teaching, have brought in enough energy, and you have enough power potential to manifest it. But this is not what happens. So this is the condition in which I find you. None of you are in agreement regarding economy. Where is there any point, any particular rule, or any particular application regarding economy in which you are all agreed? And yet you call yourselves a group and you are trying to make a group effort. It is not that you are not in agreement as to the higher purpose and the goal of your effort. But insofar as the ways and means of working it out, there isn't any working together.

To take a very simple example which you all know. If a ball team is not in agreement as to the various plays which are going to be made, it cannot possibly work together. If every member of that team is not backing the play of each one, then it is not a ball team and it cannot possibly win the game. And this is your problem.

How is it going to be worked out by a Master bringing you instruction, or any teacher talking to you? It must be worked out by yourselves, in a discussion which really means something. I should not say "a discussion"; I should say a series of discussions. Yet all of you, to a greater or lesser degree, despise discussions, because in these discussions you are faced with the problem, and it is one which is almost overwhelming in its very power and its existence.

I would say that you should lock yourselves in a room for a number of days until you have agreed upon certain points, from the top to the bottom, regardless of what it is, one subject or one activity. If you want the power, this is how you are going to have to get it. And it won't come through discussions with a few of you here and a few of you there, because again you are emphasizing the separative tendencies and difficulties within the group. It should be all together. What if you quarrel and fight? This makes no difference if you can stay together until you resolve the problem. Now, I realize that your situation does not make this possible, but nonetheless you

The Disciple and Economy

are going to have to find some way to overcome this condition. Find one thing on which you can agree upon all points: what each one is going to do, when he is going to do it, how he is going to do it, and so on. And let each one then, when he does choose his activity, and if he is accepted by the total group to carry out that activity, make sure he does it. Use the 1-2-3 or the A-B-C, because it is in physical brain appearances that you are incarnate – focused. It is here that you have to work these things out. If you would invoke the Ashramic power and magic, it will only be through a one-pointed focus.

I do not consider it either wise or beneficial to you for me to project reams of instructions to you at any time. I give you this suggestion from my perspective of your particular situation. And this applies to anything and everything you are trying to do, from running a household to a business or anything else. Where you are divided, you have no chance. If you call yourselves a member of this group, you take on group karma and you share it. Actually from my own perspective, which views you and your growth and development, your success and progress, your world of affairs which should reflect the inner success and growth of this, I think that the first decision you have to make is whether or not to be a group, really, and if so, in what areas.

I realize that my words may seem harsh to you, but they are not intended to be. It is with great love and much real heartfelt understanding that I say to you these truths. You could continue this way, you see, just as you are, manifesting pretty much the same conditions and circumstances, for the rest of the incarnation. And why should you not know when there is something very much amiss. You can then make your own choice – your own decisions.

Chapter 14

Intelligent Activity

The Organization of a Group Life,
Working out Specific Activities,
Tendency to Criticize

You have much to clarify insofar as the intelligent activity of a group is concerned. You have many ideas, many concepts, many thought-forms which have to be looked at, some of them discarded, others accepted, possibly rearranged, and definite decisions to make. Meeting for this purpose after adequate preliminary discussion would be extremely conducive to the instruction which is to follow.

Insofar as the organization of a group life is concerned, it cannot descend lower than the etheric network. However, the group life pours through the life and affairs of every one of its members and in this way does descend below the etheric network. It is only in the organization of the group body that a descent cannot be made below the etheric. And remember when we are referring to a group, we are referring now to an Ashramic group life. An Ashramic group or any part of it cannot be contained in a form below the frequency of the etheric network. However, it can use many forms, cannot be contained within them but can work through many forms below this level.

As the group is proceeding in its growth and development to find its natural forms of service expression, these forms of service expression will differ. Certain individuals will find themselves together as a group unit within the larger group because of a similarity of ray makeup, of past experience. This provides them with that common ground insofar as intelligent activity is concerned, to proceed with a specific form of expression, a specific form of activity. Now this is natural, it is normal to the growth and development of the group life. While one part of a group unit will be establishing a particular form of expression, another unit will be establishing another form. It is true that on soul levels (and I am including the incarnate soul), the entire group supports the activity and activities of the various parts of the group subjectively. But this does not mean that the total membership of the group must be concerned with the specific business activities or the specific problems involved in the many forms of expression that the group life is taking.

It means that the group unit within the larger group is contemplating a construction company or building activity, as an example, as a form of expression, and this is known by the overall group. The purpose and the goal of that particular group unit in the building of its form of expression is known, and the overall group then works to support subjectively the activity of this particular unit in the building of its form. The group will make itself available to the group unit for aid in the solution of problems which have to do with the working out of the basic principles for which the whole group stands. But the working out of specific activities or problems involved which are natural to this particular form of expression, these are not the concern of the whole group. They are the concern of the group unit.

There are a number of reasons why I am asking you to have discussions to aid in the growth and development of the group life as it does move into its natural form of expression: to bring about a greater understanding within the group regarding this particular area of development into which the group moves. There will be (not only in relationship to a construction company, as an example, but in relationship to other activities which are just as important), much negativity within the minds and the expressions of those who are not specifically concerned in this particular form of expression. Now this is also natural. This is a problem which develops along with the development of the group life in this particular phase of its growth – a problem which should be brought to the attention of the total group and should be resolved as quickly and easily as possible, so it does not grow into dimensions which can be very formidable as the group growth progresses in this way, with the rapidity that is very possible to it.

For instance, there will be those of you within the group whose background, ray makeup, and karma, have resulted in a coming together with the interest of building this particular form of expression as a service activity, both to the total group and to the humanity which the total group serves. For those of you who find yourselves attracted into this activity, and together work out the building of the activity, and resolve the natural problems which are a part of it, you find yourselves more or less with a common meeting ground. You understand, to some degree at least, the problems that you are facing.

There are some members of the group who may think that they should be attracted into this activity. They are not really, and they are concerned because they are not. There are others who will definitely not only not be attracted, but in some instances, repelled from this particular form of expression, and some who are concerned because they do not understand their right relationship with the activity. Please endeavor, and I will go further to resolve to eliminate the criticism, to eliminate not only the criticism but the negative expression of any nature regarding an effort being made by a unit newly forming within the overall group. If to you it seems that these individuals are indulging in dreams, let them dream and do not presuppose that their dreams will come to nothing simply because you yourselves are not particularly drawn to this activity and therefore do not either understand or allow its expression.

Support subjectively the activity that you find your group brothers entering into. Realize that they are following their own inner light, that they are following their own tendency as they work through the instrumentality which they have through many long ages created specifically for the purpose of service. Give them then the benefit of their own guidance. This is extremely important.

Now, at the same time, there will be other activities being contemplated by other units within the group and I consider this to be of importance. There is a real problem in group relationship in the process of development, which, as I stated previously, must be resolved. This tendency to criticize one another's activities, one another's leanings, because they do not happen to be your own, can create tremendous doubts within the minds of those who are endeavoring to move forward along that path which is right for them. If you indulge in this, then you are opposing them, actually taking the side of opposition, without either realizing it or wanting to. And this I am sure is not your intent. This also creates a tendency within some to refuse or to fear or to greatly desire not to reveal to the overall group life their particular path of expression, to withhold from the overall group life knowledge of that activity which they are either contemplating or entering. Again this not only works out as a separative factor, but it cuts off these particular units from the subjective aid which should be given every activity by the totality of the group, by the group soul.

Chapter 14

Certain activities which have been revealed as service activities, have met with a degree of rejection and as all of you realize, a certain amount of criticism; certainly then a lack of clear understanding as to what attempt was being made. It should not be a part of the attitude, it should not be a necessary part of the attitude, whether that idea is rightly or wrongly interpreted by any individual within the group life to hesitate or fear telling the overall group of its particular service plan. Because the group soul should (and that group soul includes both the overshadowing spiritual soul and the incarnating consciousness of the entire group) be moving freely through its total instrumentality, regardless of the differences of activity which are being carried out by the various members of the group.

To those of you living within a center and to those of you living outside a center, again your criticisms will have an unfortunate effect upon the success of the total activity. I then ask you to resolve, I plead with you to resolve, to eliminate these criticisms from your expressions. They are not worthy of you. They do nothing to further The Plan you seek to serve; they are destructive in their effect. They are destructive within the group body itself. And their power, because you are functioning as consciously identified souls, is much greater than you can possibly realize.

You have outgrown the need, insofar as your growth and development is concerned, for this kind of negativity. I plead with you then to lift yourselves above it, and to invoke the power of the soul to control this aspect of your form nature. I should like to point out that this instruction applies, or has reference to any other activity entered into by any one group member or unit within the total group life.

The Disciple and Economy

164

Chapter 15

Creative Economy

Conditions that Block the
Manifestation of Economy

For a period of approximately three months, or three lunar cycles, in which the energy, force, and substance which manifests outwardly as right economy when properly appropriated and put into right use by any group, will be coming your way. The major type of energy that you will be receiving will be that which relates specifically with economy, and particularly in a creative sense. By this I mean the creative economy which does build and does, in its activity, create an ever-increasing and productive economy.

There are certain conditions, if I may call them that, within the group mental body and astral body which, when orbiting or moving within the etheric, tend to block the understanding and hence the outer manifestation of economy. These conditions are contributed to by each one of you, each in his own particular way. But they constitute a real problem in that they render your functioning as a unit in this particular area of activity almost impossible. In other words, when you focus into this particular subject, you are individuals functioning as individuals rather than group brothers functioning as a group. And never at any time in your history have you been more individualized, or more representative of the individual focus and consciousness than you are right now.

The Disciple and Economy

Do not misunderstand, this is not a reprimand. Please realize that I am in no way reprimanding you or even suggesting that you do not function as individuals, but rather that you find these conditions which make it impossible for you to function, for you to apply your individual creativity, to a group effort in this particular respect.

When these conditions are overcome by any unit within the overall group life, then the problem of economy will have been solved within the group life. Certainly you are, because you are the center personnel, the natural group unit to overcome this problem.

There is much here overshadowing, much that I could project upon this subject. Yet, there is such resistance within each of you (each in your own particular prison) that to project such instruction (not an instruction telling you what to do but that which would provide you with understanding for your own formulation of a wise plan of action) would be to super-impose My will upon your own. Therefore I am stopped, barred, from such projection.

I know that this is a most difficult problem for you, a most difficult area of confusion, and I am very much in sympathy with you in your particular confusion. Yet, from my perspective, I see so clearly the light which your own soul within its Ashramic group affiliation could shine upon your path, so that within a very short period of time, through wise planning, through a unified effort, you could not only overcome the particular problem involved, but launch your service project into outer objective manifestation.

Will you take the few hints that I give you and meditate upon them?

1. That each is functioning as an individual in relation-

ship to this particular subject in one way or another.

2. That each has imprisoned himself within his own particular limitations in such a way as to block a free circulation of ideas, of concepts, of energy, force, and substance, of all of that subjective potential which, when circulating freely, would objectify in a physical appearance.

3. That each is going to have to give up some of his "pet theories" (if I may call them this) and ideas, and embrace those ideas and theories which have a more perfect relationship to the group as a whole, and to its effort at this time.

The overshadowing is present, the energies are available. There is sufficient creativity within the whole of the group, once it is a group, to manifest that which is necessary. Alone, divided, there is not.

The Disciple and Economy

Chapter 16

Science of Impression

The Function of a Group Center;

Meditating Upon Life, Quality, and Appearance;

Causal Sheath of the Ashramic Group Life

Part of the initiation process insofar as you are concerned is for you to learn, to realize and to apply the function of a group center as an invocative and evocative one, which operates, not only in the area or field of energies, but in the field of concepts and ideas, as well.

In other words, a part of your growth and development is in the development and utilization of the science of impression. In this way, you can function in times of emergency, and in areas of activity which must become your responsibility as a spiritual focal point of Ashramic consciousness and power.

You will have a good demonstration of this by the meditation you carry out for a period of two weeks, as well as your control of personality forces of a reactive nature. Usually when this subject is brought up, your energies or your forces (the devic forces) can be viewed from my own higher perspective to be moving out from each of you in a scattering and disintegrating motion, horizontally. The devic forces at work within the personality move in explosive fashion out into the etheric body of the group in different directions and patterns, so that an integrated focus of attention to that which overshadows is rendered impossible.

The Disciple and Economy

As I view you from a higher perspective, when I impact you with the concept, the energy and force of Divine Economy, I see a horizontal activity which is a scattering, a diffusion of your energies and forces, rather than an integration of them into a one-pointed focus. You will be able to maintain a control of the lower forces sufficient to bringing in the basic concept of Divine Economy with which you have been overshadowed with your meditation upon this subject.

You realize that meditation is preparatory to the approach to the full moon focus upon this particular concept, this area of activity, and this particular area of your spiritual growth and development.

After meditating upon the life, quality and appearance of the Divine Economy, which will now, because of the new concept which you have brought into your consciousness, take into account the fact that the true economy is the devic life, will constitute the major realization and contemplation of that seed thought.

Visualize this deva, impress upon him then, this concept of the manifestation of the life, quality and appearance of the Divine Economy within your economic situation as a group unit, whose responsibility is to build a group life.

And then invoke the devas to cooperate, to precipitate The Plan and realize that the devas of economy are building devas.

Work with this meditation, this technique, for the two weeks from full moon to new moon and at the same time, let the keynote of your work be precipitation, focusing then the whole of the effort into the devic life of your particular area.

All of this then is for the purpose of building, building

Chapter 16

the forms into which the group center, already constructed in mental, astral and etheric substance, can
make its appearance in the physical plane of affairs.

The concept of the center, insofar as The Plan is concerned, is that The Divine Plan insofar as the life, quality and appearance of the Divine Economy, which is the
archetype, so to speak, is already impressed within the
devic life. Your knowledge of that plan depends upon
your receptivity to impression from that deva, or upon
your receptivity to impression from within the combined
causal sheath of the Ashramic group life related to this
particular effort. You need no greater knowledge of
details at this point, for those details are only the outer
structure which will naturally coalesce around the inner. The details are worked out in sequence as The Plan
itself manifests. There is altogether too much concern
regarding the details at this particular time. Let the
concern regarding details move into its own time and
place. That concern will be confronted with you when
you are further along in the appearance. The details are
things that you will work out in their time and place.
Predetermine life, quality and appearance and the details then will fall into their right place.

When that which you respond to as being the right
place and the appearance of that which will secure it for
you (finances, in other words), come together, then you
need not hesitate. Prior to that time, keep an open
mind.

The Disciple and Economy

172

Chapter 17

Blocks

The economy must come from and through yourselves and it should not be put into administration of a group unless there is your approval to dominate, direct.

You should not even disclose the amount of money you have with you or how much money you don't have with you.

You see that any time you do disclose whether you are broke or wealthy, it is only an indication of lack of balance within your economy. If you know where that money is going, it is your prerogative to use it that way. If a large donation were given to you, I would suggest that you direct its use and in this manner you will control that area which is so difficult. If you would but learn this one problem you would have taken a great stride. This is not being secret. This is good judgment, because you know the dangers which lie within this particular area and you have seen it happen time and time again because you are involved in this. Then I think that the best thing to do should be to pay back all of those debts if you do come into a great deal of money and then make your peace with it. Take this first step and embed it upon every ounce within you that this is the proper procedure, the proper direction to take. Until you do this, you are going to find very great difficulty in adjusting to group relationships.

You do not need to feel that you must only confide with one another. This is not my point. It is where and what you are doing with your finances which is the difficult problem here, because what you do with your money is simply a supply and demand situation. Therefore, if you talk in terms of money, you are automatically putting a piece of metal on a scale and weighing it to counteract any odds which are against it. You have always looked to money as the balancer of the scale, where the purpose of it is to produce for you a growth which, if properly handled, can produce an economy within the entire group. This comes from within, not from one individual. It must come from within the area of inner nucleus outward, a flowing outward of finance. Whatever comes in must go out normally, gradually, until such time as a balance can be maintained within a group.

If you could learn this one concept, it would aid tremendously in your own growth and development, releasing much that holds the wisdom and its growth from moving forward for the group as well.

In these tiny blocks lie the misinterpretation which has been placed upon money and this, of course, is part of your problem. This is not all of it as others of any group have similar experiences. It is a pattern which all experience, but which is something that must be overcome in order to clarify for you what supply is. You make all sorts of demands, but where does your supply come from? It is not from any particular source and it is not directed to any particular source. The free flow is necessary in the establishment of a rhythm of economy.

Your block meant that it was improper for you to accept money from any source. This is my point, from *any* source. Within your own evolutionary growth and development this has been stamped upon your sense of inferiority to this particular subject. From this point let me impress upon you that those who are working with you on the other side may help you in overcoming such a definite impression within yourself. Each one of you

can relate to these personas working with you which
will enable them as well as yourselves to adjust to a
new feeling, meaning, and essence, of finance, so you
can begin to clear much of this misinterpretation from
your *every* activity.

The Disciple and Economy

Chapter 18

Wishlife and Devas

Blocks to the Movement of Economic Energy,

Conscious Evaluation of your Relationships,

The Basic Requirement of a Healthy Economy,

Polarity of Will and Intelligent Activity

There are a few areas within your personality consciousness, and I speak of all of you, which tend to block
some of that which is overshadowing because they are
in direct conflict with some of the concepts which, if
realized, could do much toward the resolution of your
particular and combined problems in economy. It is
with this subject primarily that we are concerned at
this time, because it is *vital* to the establishment of
right center function, internal and external, both in
relationship to each center itself and to the center of
synthesis.

The biggest block to the free movement of economic
energy, force, and substance is so close to mobility that
it requires but a very little more time expenditure with
a great deal of energy expenditure within that to clear it
and so free the major channels of economic movement
within the group life. Each of you contribute, each in his
own way, to that major block. Your contribution lies in
three areas:

   1. It lies in your subconscious evaluations of all
      that pertains to economic welfare, particularly in

those patterns built, developed, in the childhood and the early teenage period. This is one area in which you all contribute to the major block of which I speak.

2. Another area is in the wish life. Each one of you has formulated both consciously and unconsciously wishes of a very personal nature.

I shall not identify or define them as being either good or bad; they are not in that category. But they are wishes which, in their thought-form construction, tend to hold your supply away from you on the one hand and to either inflate or deflate your demands. Do you follow me? Now, this wish life is more conscious than unconscious. It certainly does derive from your own ego images. But it is more conscious than subconscious and can be worked with quite easily by you if you will make the attempt.

3. The third area and the one of greatest import because it is the most difficult for the soul to deal with, is in the concrete, entirely conscious but not fully understood, and this is that area of the concrete mind which constitutes your conscious evaluations of your relationships with and within the world of finance. Do you follow me?

Now, certainly, some of the thought-forms to which I refer in all three areas, will seem to bear or have little relationship to economy but they are basic to it. The thought-forms which you hold regarding yourself and your own actions, for instance, regarding your basic close primary relationships, are all influential in your economic manifestations.

The tendencies of both instrument and consciousness in little apparently unimportant areas are of vital importance. Your attitudes, feelings and thoughts, pet peeves,

Chapter 18

so to speak, all of these are vitally important and contribute to this major block. For instance, invariably in your discussions of this subject you finally get around to the subject of how to solve the problems of supply; that is, how to get more supply, if I may put it in these terms. And here, in this area, you are extremely limited, so limited that you build the block much larger because you convince yourself over and over in every discussion, that certain manifestations certainly are not likely to occur. Do you follow me?

You have not realized, as yet, the tremendous possibilities which are very close and which attend the effort that you are setting out to make. Therefore, I ask you to expand your consciousness to remove some of the limitations and the barriers there regarding this, to view and accept some of these possibilities.

Certain attitudes, thought-forms, fears, and dependencies, blind you to the setting into motion of manifesting that energy, force, and substance which will result in an outward physical manifestation of supply. These are the areas in which discussion would be of tremendous benefit if you can direct your discussion into areas wherein your thinking has been limited. The basic requirement of the building of a healthy, creative economy is *resource*. It can be of a mental frequency, which will then require its movement down into astral, etheric and finally physical frequencies in order to manifest. It can be of mental and astral; it can be mental, astral and etheric. It can be mental, astral, etheric, and physical, or any of these. All that is required is *resource*.

Now, in the effort you are entering into, you have a resource. It is the right directional movement, the organization of that, and its movement through whatever frequencies are lacking in its development, that is required now.

The Disciple and Economy

Being resourceful is, in a sense, almost a misnomer. It simply means that you, being resourceful, are to cognize or realize resources at hand. What I am referring to are the actual resources which are yours, which you have, which could be developed into a healthy, creative (and creative, of course, is vitally important to you) economy. Now, as I said, a resource can be of a mental nature. When it is, it requires a movement down into the astral, the etheric, and the physical before it can manifest. It can be of an astral nature and require, then, the mental frequency, the etheric, and the physical frequencies to develop it. These resources you have in abundance. You have these resources. They only need development, and it is only the limitations within your thinking which make it difficult for you to set into motion the direction of energy, force, and substance which develop these resources.

It is a tendency of the human being to maintain the status quo, to do things according to the pattern already established. He sees the ruts that have been established and looks so concentratedly into those ruts that he does not see the obvious new fields, the new patterns and the ground within which these patterns can be established. The entire effort will be in relationship to economy. The focus will be here. Now I would say one thing about this which I consider to be of importance at this time. Desire, astral magnetic power, never created any economy. It never attracted money; it never will. It takes the will energy to move economic energy, force, and substance. Therefore, this focus of attention, this focused intent into the resolution of the economic problem both personally and group-wise, will do more to move the major block than anything that has happened previously.

One or two individuals cannot resolve the group problems of economy by themselves. It will require the concentrated will energy of more than just one in the group to resolve the group problem of economy. It could be

180

Chapter 18

done by four of you. It does not matter what activities that two of you are engaged in, one activity and two of you together, or all of you in different activities for that matter, if the will is focused into the resolution of these particular problems. It is the positive polarity of the will and the negative polarity of intelligent activity which results in outer manifestation. Actually, you would have my approval if you focused the will in this direction regardless of the time involved and maintained that focus until these problems have been resolved. It is impossible to focus the intent in order to initiate something into, for instance, the training of students and at the same time resolve the problems of economy. In other words, if you are going to initiate on an economic level, the will must come into this level. Then after it is established, after the motion of energy, force, and substance has been set into its orbit, then the will can be turned from it to carry forward other activities.

Take one step at a time. That is why some in a group have done as much as they have done in an economic sense, because their will focus has been focused in this direction, not necessarily in the most productive manner, but certainly far more productive than when the will is not focused in that direction.

Resident students are very much ready with what I shall call minor indications or tendencies, which stem from experience. That past may be very occluded at this time, and yet it will take but the strength of the soul alignment, a clearing out of confusion resulting from this incarnation's experience which may have been most difficult, the removal of obsessing factors to bring to the fore, to bring to the front, to bring into those personas and their equipment, much wisdom gained over past incarnations. They are extremely likely (if I may use this term, insofar as a center is concerned), and can become one of the functioning disciples in the center, if all goes well with their development. They could be close to a type of command (I am referring to the point of soul development and past experience) over the elemental forces of the earth. This is why, for this kind of a center, some students could be particularly well fitted, and I would not curb or in any way deter them from their need and love of work outdoors, because this may be their path, and it is very good. Students can be of tremendous benefit insofar as the center function itself is concerned. Writing will help to clear away the confusion. Once that confusion has been cleared out and they recognize their relationship to the subhuman kingdoms and the service, the path of service which is theirs, they will be or can be, potentially have the ability to be, the disciple, insofar as any center is concerned, in command of the devic forces, insofar as the subhuman kingdoms in nature are concerned. Do not forget that the devic life of all kingdoms in nature, in any center, serve as a part of the center personnel, a part of the center focus. And so carry the energy of that center into their particular frequency and distribute it throughout their entire kingdom. Just as the humans distribute energy throughout the body of humanity, so then does the plant deva within the center itself – so do they distribute the energy coming into the center throughout the plant kingdom, so do the animals throughout the animal kingdom, and the mineral throughout the mineral kingdom. This is a part of a perfect center function and there must be a disciple or more in command of these devic forces.

The consciousness of the overshadowing Divine Plan is the consciousness of the Christ. The Plan in its form nature, that is, in its activity aspect as form, is of the highest order of deva available to the human kingdom on this planet. It is the deva, or the order of devas, referred to as the vestures or the risen Holy Ghost Aspect. This then, is the overshadowing Divine Plan as held in focus – the consciousness of Christ within the mind of

Christ, that mind being the risen Holy Ghost Aspect within the Mind of Christ, the form nature, of The Divine Plan Itself.

Next, we have the focal point of consciousness which is the ashramic group life, with the etheric light body of the Planetary Logos as the form nature or the deva of the ashramic group life.

The key to contact with and control of the devas who constitute your form nature lies in this concept of the consciousness establishing itself in a focal point behind the breath. The fact is that it is the nature of the form to breathe; it is not the nature of the consciousness to breathe. Devas are controlled via the appropriation of their breath; it is the direction of their life toward the manifestation of a given purpose. The completion of the alignment, or the completion of the circuit which is the completion of the alignment can be made only via the appropriation by the consciousness of the life of the substantial forces on the lowest plane of appearance and the direction of that life back to the overshadowing source or the origin of the alignment.

You are more than a soul. You are a part of The Divine Plan in manifestation, and it is as that Divine Plan in manifestation that protective power and presence of the Christ is invoked around you. Such protection not only throws a light upon your spiritual path of endeavor both in consciousness and the outer experience which you must enter, through which you must pass, but it also screens, so to speak, those forces impacting your instrument horizontally, screening out all that would impact you which is out of harmony with your expression of The Divine Plan.

The Disciple and Economy

Chapter 19

Ask and Ye Shall Receive

Let Go of the Old Ways

Master John:

I would like to comment on how apropos is the meditation upon the concept and its suggestion, "ask and ye shall receive", in an unemployment office where you are asking for money to sustain you until you can get another job while you are looking for one. It is very interesting that you would find yourself in this position, no? What does "ask and you shall receive" mean? And this is a very good point for it has a direct relationship to much of that which I was speaking to you about just a moment ago. In the first place, "ask and ye shall receive" means primarily to ask from that point of identification which is, in this instance, the Conscious Soul Incarnate. As a Conscious Soul Incarnate, particularly in your position (by this I mean the realization which you have made and the effort you are making, along the lines of these realizations) you cannot honestly go into an unemployment office and ask for (as the Conscious Soul Incarnate) money to sustain you while you are looking for another job. This is not a complete and clear alignment.

Actually, what is happening, the soul has seen a concept and is attempting to embody that concept, but is afraid to let go of the old ways or the old thought-forms. This is really quite important. There is nothing wrong with using the old thought-forms, but use them when they serve your purpose. If you use them, do not confuse issues. In other words, if you conceive an idea, if you grasp a concept and relate to it your particular situation and circumstance, and if the light indicates a course of action new and strange to you and utterly different from which you would have followed previously, then you must dare to either follow it, or follow the old path and think about the new one. When you confuse the two, you are going to manifest the confusion. In other words, you've got to take the action that is the true action of your conviction whatever that conviction may be. This is where you have made a mistake.

To the Conscious Soul Incarnate this would be unthinkable. If you will really think about it, particularly when this does not serve the purpose which the conscious soul is endeavoring to manifest, the Conscious Soul Incarnate simply would not do this. This would not be intelligent activity. So you are going to move along a path, and take a course of action which is new and strange, unfamiliar, but which has been indicated by your own spiritual light. Then, my Brother, dare to walk along it and do not look back lest you find yourself like that character you know, who became a pillar of salt.

A decision has to be followed by intelligent activity indicated by that decision. The reason I said "dare to follow the new path or follow the old one and think about the new one" is that in the first place the disciple begins to grasp higher laws and the concepts which have relationship to the higher laws. He grasps then a course of action which seems possible but very improbable to him and it takes meditation and consideration before he is really ready to take that path. It not only takes this, but it takes failure following the old path, you know. He has to fail many times before he is ready and willing to move along the new one. Thinking about the new one will expand his consciousness while he is following the old path. It will bring him greater understanding – it

Chapter 19

will not manifest what he is seeking to manifest by taking the new path. But it will bring him to a readiness so when the day comes, he can make the decision and move according to that decision.

You can talk about it, meditate about it, dream about it, all you want to and it will not manifest until you take action. The subjective is objectified through its focus within the physical instrument and the activity in which that physical instrument is engaged. Remember that the individual lives within a network of relationships and within that network there are many centers. It is only through his activity in the physical instrument, with the purpose held in mind, that he can objectify that which is subjective. It is necessary to take the action indicated by your purpose and your goal within the physical instrument in order to manifest it.

As disciples you are learning — feebly, yes. The learning process is really much more rapid than you realize when you use your mental bodies. The time will come, when as the Conscious Soul Incarnate, focused within the cave, you will at will enter into the mental body and use it for the purpose of creating a thought-form, of directing energy, of communicating on mental levels with other minds, etc. What you do there will register in the brain, yes; but what you do will be free from the limitations of the brain.

The Disciple and Economy

Chapter 20

Laws

The Master Deva of Economy;

Right Use of Energy, Force, and Substance;

Formulating Laws to Govern Economy;

Transmitting the Laws to the Devas

In order to manifest any outer appearance, regardless of what it is, there must be formulated laws which govern the activity of the devas in relationship to that manifestation. This is a part of ceremonial magic, and it is why the Seventh Ray is defined as ceremonial magic or Divine Law and Order.

Any organization proceeds under law.

I have described the mechanics involved in the devic response, the devic activity, the intelligent activity which manifests an outer picture of a focused intent.

Now what command does the deva understand? Laws, formulated laws are the framework given to the deva which makes it possible for him, on his own, with his own intelligence, to proceed with the building process.

For instance, you understand the mechanics in relationship to the devic activity, and I am going to repeat the mechanics so that you will be clear as to what I am referring.

The Disciple and Economy

The Master Deva of Economy is a deva who is, in a sense, the overlord or the deva in command of all of the lesser devas of economy, which are specifically related to the group life. Also, the Master deva is overlord of all those lesser devas which *can* be specifically related to the group life, and this is an important point. There are many devas of economy within the environment, many devas of economy within the world of affairs, which have not yet been attracted into a relationship with the group life through lack of intelligent activity, through lack of that devic action which would have attracted them.

The Master Deva of Economy, then, the Commander-in-Chief, so to speak, of the economic forces of the group life, those presently within the group life and those who are potentially related to the group life, receives the focused intent of the group. Now that focused intent is formulated into specific stated laws.

The Master Deva receives that intent, organizes those forces under Him, gives them their direction — and so long as the intent is maintained, so long as that focused intent of the group is maintained, so long as it does not receive an attack, so to speak, from any part of the group consciousness, (and this may come as a surprise to you, devic forces being as recipient of attack as is the consciousness) so long as the focused intent is not counteracted, or is not detracted from by any part of the group consciousness — then the Master Deva, using this focused intent as His blueprint, sets into motion, organizes His lower forces, sets into motion that which will out-picture the focused intent.

It is the passage of the intent, the impression of the intent upon the Master Deva, the communication between consciousness and Master Deva which is of importance. And this proceeds under law. The devic forces understand; it is their nature to understand law. If the

190

group formulates a principle, if the group grasps, for instance, a principle of economy, and formulates that principle into a law, a law which will govern the economic life and affairs of the group, or will govern one phase of it, then that law is communicated to the Master Deva.

There are three basic laws of economy, if you will remember, which have been refined and clarified in the *Disciple and Economy* Introductory lesson.

Now let us take for instance, just one of these basic laws which is right use of that which you have. The first job, if I may use this term, for any group of this kind, as it visualizes these plans it would materialize, is to transmit to the Master Deva of Economy, its Master Deva of Economy, the first basic Law of Economy: "Right use of all of the energy, force, and substance — right use of all of the energy, force, and substance which is subjective and of the energy, force, and substance which is objective." This takes in economic forces of the group.

So the first law to transmit then to the Master Deva is that all use of these economic forces will proceed under Divine Guidance, will proceed in Divine Law and Order so that such use will be right use.

Now any principle can be formulated into a law. That law is then transmitted to the Master Deva of Economy so that every time an impression is given to the Master Deva of Economy and is qualified in Divine Law and Order; the Master Deva knows the framework of law within which He can work. He knows it because you have transmitted that law to Him.

Every organization must formulate — whether it is a subjective organization, an esoteric one, or an outer objective one — it must formulate its laws.

The Disciple and Economy

Because any organized activity proceeds under law; the law is the dynamic. For instance, you have formulated a law which will govern this group in an economic sense, which states that every individual member of the group shall have at all times whatever economy is necessary to fulfill his needs. Then the Master Deva of Economy works in His manifestation under that law. And this is how change takes place. This is how the disciple, particularly the disciple working in a group, this is how the group imposes a new rhythm; this is how the group imposes change; this is how the group alters the present set of conditions and circumstances which are the outworking, which are the manifestation of karmic factors in the past. This is how the conscious group, the self-conscious group, alters those conditions, changes them, and comes into control, comes into control of his devic life and affairs.

For instance, if you at this point, can agree upon one basic Law of Economy – which will govern the economic forces of the group life, can formulate that law, concisely, clearly and then communicate the law to the Master Deva – you will have taken a major step in the solution of that problem of economy which has been with you, actually, from the time you moved onto the path of discipleship.

In other words, now as a group, you understand what you are really working with – Seventh Ray organization. Agree upon one law which is to govern the economic life and affairs of the group itself, and then, as a group, focus the intent to the Master Deva. In other words, give Him this law. Do this now and then proceed to formulate those laws which will govern the economic life of the group. If you can do this during this period, you will have given the devas of economy through the Master Deva something with which to work. No government can function without law and you, in a sense, are building a government.

Chapter 20

You see, law must come before the building of the structure. For the structure cannot go up before there is a law and order which governs the building of any structure.

So now the task before you is to find those laws, formulate these laws which incorporate the principles that you as a group intend to manifest, to live by. After you have established this framework of law, then you can pass to your deva the picture of whatever you wish to manifest and He can work.

I would like to refer you back to the theme of this particular cycle of activity, which is Service, and to remind you that this is — the type of work you are doing now, that which you have just completed today as a first step — is real service activity. You are establishing the coordinates within which you can function, can live, and can achieve that growth and development which is potential to you during this particular incarnation. This is real work, and it is my hope that you will be able to find the time to follow it up, complete it, so that by the next new moon you have established a framework of law within which the devic life of your economy can proceed with its intelligent activity and the carrying out of your purpose and plan.

This technique, this methodology, applies to any cooperative relationship between consciousness and devic life. The first step is the formulation of the law. The second step is the transmission of that law, via communication to the deva involved.

The Disciple and Economy

Chapter 21

Share your Energy

Invoke and Wield Spiritual Power;

Synthesis of Light, Love, and Power;

Manifestation of The Divine Plan;

The White or the Black Magician;

A New Kind of Faith;

The Path of Initiation and

The Path of Illumination

Always to a greater or lesser degree (and I might say that in certain areas where a group has functioned during the immediate past, it has been with greater degree), you are extremely conscious of that which you are receiving in the way of energies, in the way of experience. Of course, you do not receive experience, but you tend to think that you do; you think in the old pattern of the persona prior to discipleship, but seldom do you think about what you are giving to humanity by the fact of your presence within the body of humanity, both individually and collectively. There is much meditation entered into to manifest this or that or the other, for yourselves or your service activity; much meditation entered into to manifest this or that kind of an economy, and yet there is very little true occult use made of the economy which is yours in this spiritual sense.

The disciple is radiatory; the most powerful activity into

The Disciple and Economy

which he enters is radiatory activity. He is constantly, if he is focused and he is functioning as a disciple, giving in the energy sense to those with whom he comes into physical contact (that is, via his feelings and his thoughts). If the members of a group could give a little more conscious attention to giving, to radiating those conditions, those experiences of growth, the energies which underlie those forms which you feel you yourselves need to give to the humanity you seek to serve, you would find that much in the way of economic difficulty would clear up. I have many times discussed this concept with you in many different ways. We have come to it from many different approaches. I ask you how often during the day, during the hour, do you as an individual and as a member of a group, working within the effort of the Hierarchy, give light, love and spiritual power to the human beings with whom you come in contact? Particularly would I speak to you of giving spiritual power. Have you considered this? In your contact with others, those who manifest need, have you considered the giving of spiritual power to them? Do you follow my meaning? It is necessary to invoke into your own instrumentality and attempt to wield spiritual power. It is likewise necessary and important to invoke into your instrumentality and endeavor to wield Divine Love, Divine Law and Order, or any other of the energies which are yours for the taking. It is of vital importance and necessary for you to give these energies, give freely and continuously to the humanity, individually and collectively, whom you seek to serve.

Any higher energy which could be of use to you could be of just as much use to any other member of humanity, to any other human being. In other words, what spiritual power will do for you, it will do for anyone else. If the individual with whom you come in contact has a problem (and who does not?) that problem is an evolutionary one, always. Every problem has behind it the Divine Purpose of aiding the evolutionary growth and development of humanity. Realize this: with every problem, whether it is your own or another's, spiritual power would aid you as a disciple in working through one of your problems. So will it aid any other human being in working through one of his problems. In fact, it is the right synthesis of light, love, and power which will help the immediate problem of a vehicle now, today, and aid the manifestation of The Divine Plan as it relates to that particular individual and as it relates to his point of evolutionary growth and development. Give him this synthesis and in those cases where it is obviously seen that a specific energy is needed, focus the attention on the giving of that energy. You aid, you serve the consciousness, the evolving consciousness of humanity. You can appropriate the energy that your brother does not even know exists. This you can do because you are disciples, because you cognize that energy; you are aware of it.

Appropriate it then. Do not use it just for yourselves. Do not use it just in the working out of your own problems. Give it first to those with whom you come in daily contact. Realize that that contact, because you are disciples, is for a specific reason. You have so placed yourselves in relationship to the Christ that you ask to serve. You are given daily the opportunities to serve particularly in your contacts. Every moment of time that you spend in appropriating energies and wielding them in some activity, whether it be personal or group, but having to do with yourselves, spend the same amount of time in working for others in transmitting the energy and giving it specifically.

Always give the synthesis of light, love, and power. Realize that that synthesis is the coming together of these three energies in that perfect synthesis which is the precipitating agent of The Plan. Then, for those who perceive, who are aware of a need within any situation for a specific energy in addition to the synthesis, appropriate and give that Divine energy to your brother.

Always qualify all activity in Divine Law and Order. This protects the individual. Understand that any higher energy which you appropriate and give to another individual can only be used by that individual according to Divine Purpose so long as he is unconscious or unaware of that energy. When he is aware, when he is conscious of it, then he himself is capable of appropriation and can then appropriate and direct it as he so wills. In such an instance it is important to qualify, to direct, to place the energy, so to speak, in the jurisdiction of the Soul within the instrument. In such a case, one should visualize the alignment between the overshadowing Soul and the incarnate consciousness within the head. For those daily contacts that you make with average humanity, individuals who are unaware of the existence of such energy, it will follow the Divine Purpose for which it was intended.

All energy is directed. The activity of any energy has been directed by some mind, by a consciousness functioning within the mind. Insofar as average humanity is concerned, very seldom has the energy which is manifesting been directed consciously by his mind. He gives it individual tone and color. If you will notice, all experience falls into certain classifications and humanity shares in the experience of the whole. The thought-forms directing the energies within the human family are directed by either the White or the Black magician. They work through the individuals according to the point of development of those individuals and their tendencies, that is, their receptivity. At this point, one must differentiate between imposition of will and the wielding of influence.

That lower state of consciousness with which you have so much difficulty, that tremendous group life which constitutes the hidden subjective personality aspect, are

Chapter 21

only apparent obstacles to the growth and development of the Soul itself. The true Divine Power lies in the higher realms of consciousness. Regardless of where a man might be in awareness and understanding, if within his heart there is love and aspiration, and within his mind there is that need to know, and out of the two there is some desire to be of service, then this man can invoke into his life and affairs that higher power which will make possible his conscious service to The Plan.

There is necessarily a great deal of attention given to these things which constitute obstacles to growth, obstacles to illumination. But it can be known, realized, and recognized by each one of you, that these obstacles (even this hidden subjective and powerful dweller on the threshold) is as nothing in the face of a higher power.

You have been given meditation techniques, and you have been given the technique of the Great Invocation, which makes possible your alignment with the higher state of consciousness, with the higher power. It is possible, then, for you to invoke that power into service to The Plan.

I refer to a power which makes it possible to illumine, to expand your consciousness. I refer to a very subtle power which works from within the consciousness to achieve growth.

You can invoke this power once you have grasped it and once you have aligned with it. Relate it to consciousness, never to the form. Its use can only be applied to the consciousness. If, for instance, you would incorporate into your own response mechanism, into your life and affairs, some concept of Truth, but there is within your consciousness the limitation which as a result causes you to manifest the polar opposite of the concept of truth, that to which you aspire, then it is possible for you to invoke the higher consciousness, that higher

The Disciple and Economy

Divine Power to work within your consciousness, to illumine, to bring light, to show you where your limitation is, where it is and how to overcome it, through a simple expansion of consciousness which includes rather than excludes truth.

What I am attempting to give you is a new kind of faith. In the past, this faith which was taught related to the form, related to things material rather than to things spiritual. If you have faith you can be healed in body, etc. There is a recognition which is possible to you of that Christ consciousness which works within all consciousness to produce growth.

It is the invocation into the brain consciousness, into the indwelling consciousness of that which is just as present within the human entity as is the personality aspect. It is just as present as the subjective, the hidden persona.

One of the reasons why this particular concept is difficult is because it has to do with a different path from that with which you are familiar. During this period of human evolution the many paths of approach merge and become one. These many paths will be merged so that you will become conscious of not one way but many ways, which, as you synthesize those many ways, become again one way. There is a path which the consciousness accepts and travels, which is a long slow process of evolution via conflict. There is another path which supersedes or transcends the long slow process, in that the consciousness need not fight, so to speak, for his illumination. He need only align with it and receive it. To travel one or the other of these two particular paths alone is impossible today. They have to be merged. Therefore, you receive this concept which can be applied along with the other concepts which you are now using. While you will give your attention to the Path of Initiation, you will also give your attention to

Chapter 21

the Path of Illumination and in combining these two you will make possible (and I refer not to you alone, but to all disciples) the Path of Initiation of human consciousness.

Application of it in the daily life and affairs is made possible through the invocation of the higher power into intelligent activity. If it is possible for you to recognize, to accept the tremendous power of the subjective personality, then should it not be possible for you to accept the greater power of the overshadowing spiritual Soul, the power of that spiritual Soul to incarnate into that vehicle which has been dedicated to it?

As you go about your activities, using the Great Invocation, align with the concept. Do not strain to receive it or to reach it. Align with it and then via a relaxed but an alert receptivity, permit the concept to enter into your consciousness.

This is a most difficult concept to transmit. Consider a network of light which is representative of a state of consciousness upon the earth, a state of consciousness which is receptive to a greater light, a light which is so penetrating that as it enters into that network of light it transforms it and in transforming, alters the apparent conditions in which humanity lives.

What I am attempting to give you is the possibility of the establishment of a receptivity to light, light which is not only illumining but is transforming, a power which works from within the consciousness to achieve growth, to expand your consciousness.

You are entering into a period which is common to all disciples, one which all disciples experience cyclically and of which they gradually learn to make use. The instruction which has been projected and of which you have partaken has produced within the totality of your consciousness that activation which results in conflict. You are beginning now that therapeutic process which every disciple on the path must undergo, which he must experience as he is brought up into the light of his Soul, and every aspect, every area of his consciousness revealed in that light. This will pass. As you move from the valley up onto the mountain top, you will have attained the freedom of consciousness, depth of understanding and a capacity to love which you have not in the past experienced. You are seeing all that which lies within you which has to be transmuted to service to the Christ. As you experience this cyclic valley, realize that you have the protection of the Hierarchy and the protection of the Christ. Call upon that protection and at the same time, realize that you are now treading the Path of Initiation consciously and with intent.

Sit back, watch and observe. Transmute whenever and wherever possible, and love. Particularly you must love those areas of consciousness within yourself which you would hate. For this is the coming revelation. Treat every area of your consciousness with love of the Christ. Let your direction be one-pointed, let it be toward the Christ.

And now, you have before you a very tremendous opportunity to be of service and to prove yourselves as a group. I call upon the group to rally around each member of the group, to provide compassion, understanding, strength and love which will make it possible for each to pass safely and easily through this period of growth. Place yourself within the group, within its consciousness, within its love and its understanding. Realize during the coming days that you are not only making progress individually, but that your experience is enabling the group to progress as well, so that in this you are serving just as you would serve if you were able to manifest the understanding and the freedom of consciousness which you have known previously.

Chapter 22

Group Finance

Individual Karma Absorbed Into Group Karma,

Money a Crystallized Form of Third Ray,

The First Law of Economy,

Time is a Part of Your Economy

Just how responsible is a group, for instance, for one another's finances? A very pointed question if I may say so and a question which is important. I am going to answer that question with another question. Do you, any of you, understand the import, the meaning of the group life, of group effort? The same question was asked, "Am I my brother's keeper?" It is the responsibility of every member of the group for the life and affairs of every other member of the group in every area of that life and affairs. You all share in varying degrees, of course, one another's responsibility to work out those problems of humanity with which you are individually (perhaps in small group units) and collectively involved. You are no more responsible for one person's finances than you are for any other member of the group, or than they are for yours. Once the group can begin to understand this, then the solution to the problems which focus in and through the group membership will be more easily resolved.

Remember, individual karma is exchanged for group karma, it is absorbed into group karma. On a practical level, what does this mean? The problems which any disciple, any member of a group, brings into focus, requires the united effort of the overall group to solve. That solution is brought into relationship with the problem via meditation. It is directed into manifestation as the manifest solution via the subjective efforts of the group, and it is grounded via the objective efforts of the group.

This problem of finances would not be a problem, would not be present, if it were not contributed to by every member of a group in the handling of group economy. Money is but a crystallized form of Third Ray energy, an outer reflection, an outer picture of the economy of energy, force, and substance. According to your use of your economy will it manifest in the outer life and affairs a healthy or an unhealthy economy. This is a difficult concept, yet it is a law of group life.

It is most difficult to project instruction to you because immediately when I project the concept, the connotations within your mind rise to completely cloud and befog the entire issue. The moment I say that you are responsible for one another's finances, you become so immersed in your financial difficulties that you do not understand what I am saying to you. I am not telling you to put all your money, for instance, into one pot. This is not the answer or the solution. I am telling you that your use of your economy is reflected outwardly in the group in a very unhealthy and unstable, confused and chaotic, economic (with the financial condition as but a minor part of that) condition.

The first law, basic Law of Economy, which has to be wielded by the disciple who is endeavoring to live according to higher law is that of right use. When I speak of the word "right", I am not referring to any moralities. I speak of right use of that which is at hand, of that which is immediately at hand, right use according to the law. What does the Law of Economy deal with?

Chapter 22

Basically it deals with manifestation, does it not? It is the economy of the substantial forces of an organized life that results in manifestation, one kind of manifestation or another. According to the right use, under Law (right meaning according to the Laws of Economy of that which you already possess), will manifest The Plan you seek to serve. This is the first law. Economy is created out of that which is immediately at hand. The energy of the mind, the force of the astral body, the substance of the etheric body, plus all of those forms within your particular jurisdiction at your command, are put into right use, made to serve The Plan to which you think, and feel, and say that you are dedicated. Then the economy itself recreates whatever is needed for the next step in the manifestation. If that which is at hand is not put into right use, right according to the law, you have immediately a breakdown in your economy.

This law has its application in many, many areas. I have stressed over and over the right use of your mental energy, your astral force and your etheric substance. Of this you are aware, and I am sure you all know wherein you failed to apply this law in these areas. Through wrong thinking, through wrong emotional direction of astral force you are manifesting a negative condition. Is this right use of the law? It is the wrong utilization of the etheric substance, wrong according to your purpose. Let us come now down to more basic factors (correction, not more basic, there is nothing more basic than the use of your mental energy, your astral force and your etheric substance). Let us come down to more obvious and easily understood factors. How do each one of you use your time? This is a part of your economy. This is a tremendous area of error within any group life insofar as the right use of that which is immediately at hand. Some mis-apply here more than others. Some contribute to the group problem much more than do others, but this is just one area where wrong use will result in an outer condition with which you are familiar.

The Disciple and Economy

Now look at some of the other forms. Look at the supply which is immediately at hand. Each one individually, to what use does he put his training? To what use does he put his relationships? Do they serve The Plan? To what use does he put his home? To what use (and, of course, "use" indicates "uses") does he put his speech, his automobile, his bank account, etc.? To what use does he put himself? All of these are basic factors. The law applies on many different levels of understanding. It is according to the depth of the understanding of the disciple that he must apply the law. The initiate can initiate certain manifestations which will maintain themselves, but the probationer who has not put into right use what he has at hand (or even the accepted disciple who is weak in this area) cannot. For instance, if you overstep, imbalance your finances (that bad word again) before you have put all that which you have immediately at hand into right use, you throw your outer economy into an imbalance. You can expect to reap the karmic effects of this. You can expect financial difficulties. It is very simple. It is common sense. If you burden yourself before you have learned to command the energy, force, and substance of your own instrumentality, for instance, those forms which you have created with debts which you have no visible means of paying, then you can expect, naturally, to find yourselves in financial difficulty. On the other hand, you put that which is immediately at hand into the best economic use. What do we mean by best economic use? If your energy, force, and substance and those forms at your command are organized and made to serve the Divine Purpose and Plan to which you are dedicated, then you will find very quickly that you will resolve this problem.

You utilize common sense.

Once a group solves this particular problem, it will have rendered a very great service to humanity, particularly in this time.

Chapter 22

When the disciple has learned to put into right economic use that which is immediately at hand, he has resolved the problem of finances once and for all.

The disciple who has learned to put that which is immediately at hand into right economic use will never find himself without whatever finances are necessary at any given moment, never. It will not be necessary for him to appear even to create an imbalance.

This will not be true for the disciple who has not learned, who is learning. Therefore, he finds himself in this situation when his faith in The Plan, sometimes his personal desires and ambitions (usually a combination of both), have caused him to place himself in a very difficult financial position. As he puts into right use that which is immediately at hand, he will work his way out of the problems, the apparent impossibilities. This requires complete honesty, individually and collectively, because every member of the group will manifest group error as well as group embodiment. Every member will manifest according to his share in the group life, according to his degree of functionality, and how much effort he puts into his own function.

Money is a form, a physical object, which every disciple has to learn to utilize. Money symbolizes all of the separated desires, separated ambitions, the wish life of every human being on the planet today. This is the power of the persona, to manifest, so it interprets its desires and ambitions. Therefore, it is a difficult lesson to learn to appropriate and put into right use this particular form. No group is without its wish life.

It involves all of the economy which money simply symbolizes. Everything in this world, your physical plane of appearance, has its monetary value.

Time is a very important factor here, because your time

is measured today in this world of physical appearances by monetary values.

I should like to further clarify the meaning of the right use of time. Your energy, force, and substance moves into time and space. There it manifests in objective form according to your use of that energy, force, and substance and your use of time for coordination of the two. You must learn to wield time as surely as you wield any law, as surely as you wield any energy, as surely as you wield any instrument, for this is what it is, an instrument.

Chapter 23

Student Supply

The Nucleus Group, Personal Training,
The Student Will Supply that Which is Necessary

Your purpose throughout this incarnation has been to bring into manifestation a plan, a Divine Plan for humanity. Your service has been a dedication to this as you have been able to grasp it. We know your problems, of course you realize this. We are very close to you. And yet, We in the greater awareness are able to see past the personality worries, inadequacies, and therefore can see a much larger picture than as yet you are able to recognize. Our work has been a dedication to The Plan, to which you have dedicated your entire life, your entire incarnation. We are of the opinion that if you will recognize what is being attempted in this short span in which you will be working, and recognize those who are related to you in the physical body, a tremendous amount of teaching is going to be made available through you. The personality conflicts and the various problems seem very immaterial to Us on this level where We function.

I know that within your own area of growth these problems are extremely important. We do not shun them or make them immaterial, seem of no importance, for they are. But, for your growth and development that has taken place up to this point, there is much that you are not aware of that is taking place. The pattern which has been put into operation is being formed into a permanent structure which can be worked through by incarnate individuals with whom you are associated and by Us where We function. The overall pattern is forming to the extent that very shortly it will be apparent to you. The other members who are not yet in physical contact with you are being drawn into your frequency, into juxtaposition with you so that very shortly these individuals will make their presence known to you. It is important to draw these individuals into your circle to bring them into their function and to recognize the place they play within your service activities.

You are to attract to the nucleus group, those who are nucleus group, wherever you are. As soon as they come into your sphere of influence into group work, there will be a great expansion, because, you understand, that each functions in his own particular frequency and yet is related to the others so that the attraction will seal the ring and let the full force of that which is to come into incarnation manifest. This is your main purpose, not only as a center but as an attractive force reaching out to those with whom you are related. I might add, those with whom you are beginning now to relate are working to bring those individuals, those in incarnation who are nucleus group members but who have not yet found the way, to you. They are helping to help you attract them.

A piece of property need not be purchased, although for your own desires this would satisfy and give you a security you do not now possess. It is more important for you than it would be for Us. The training of the students is very important to Us. The rehabilitation, the recapitulation of those whom you attract is of great importance to Us for the student training at this time, not that a great many people will be attracted into the area for training. Personal training is the keynote at this particular time and I think this would answer your question regarding the continuance of your property after you go out of incarnation. The training of these people will begin to create for you the needed equipment and buildings as the individuals manifest for that training. It is again a matter of supply, demand and training to create a demand. In other words, training of these individuals now will attract others who are ready for their training. The cooperation involved in thus reaching the function of each one of these will build your buildings. If you can wait this long, then do so. Think small in terms of individuals, not large groups.

You see that if you thought in terms of large buildings and training many, many students, attracting many into your retreat, you would take on the responsibility of feeding them, housing them, and here again you would be taking on a particular problem which is not your own.

If you begin to think in terms of feeding large numbers, you are defeating your own purpose. Your purpose is not to feed large numbers, it is to train those who can feed the large numbers.

When the time comes that you have need for larger quarters, then the people who need the larger quarters will manifest them. I am not trying to tell you what you should do, but I am indicating the way in which you will find the least involvement for yourselves and you begin now to start a precedent that the people who come to you must find their own facilities in order to receive their training. If it be a group effort to rent a building wherein you would train them, or whether you take them into your home, should be of no concern to you at this time.

The manner in which you begin is important. You establish a precedent in this way, that the students if they desire training, will find their training center, either a small office or within their own homes. It is not your responsibility to rent or buy a very large place at this time, for it would defeat your purpose. The student himself will supply that which is necessary for his own training. You see you are beginning now to understand the supplying of the students needs. He supplies his needs. You supply his training.

You will find that the student can always make adjustments if he knows the pattern which has been established. If you take many into your home, the new ones coming in naturally will expect this. But if you would go for instance to another's home for a period of time during the day and train him there, this would take away the need for the home where you live to be used for this purpose. I think you would find that as soon as this begins to happen that the student would find the means by which to have an easier process.

I am not indicating that this should be the path you take; however, I am indicating now how supply of the student is made available to him. You, in other words, are cutting off his supply by manifesting for him his training center, his place of training.

It does not mean that when someone asks you for help you do not give it in your own home. This is not what I am saying. I am saying that the supply of the student will be freed if you will take this attitude at all times without causing a misrelationship. To establish it will change the flow of supply for the student and of course it will change for you, also.

I am saying only to proceed on faith. This is all that I can give you and you have proceeded thus far, let it continue. I understand the difficulties and yet I see as I said a great deal of growth taking place within every group so that the point which I can give you to hold onto is this one latch string. The other members of the group will come in their own time, but a much shorter time than it was, much shorter. This I give you to hold in mind.

As you grow, so does the opposition. The lack of cooperation from others is only an indication of the inferiority which they feel in their own work when they contact such a high frequency of understanding, of wisdom, which you are carrying with you. They at first are open and receptive and yet when they begin to feel the impact which you are making, the reaction takes place. The frequency of the Thought-form Presentation of the Wisdom itself, the background, the looking into the future, the whole of it, is so much of an impact in the world today. This is why the work is seemingly at a standstill. It is only a matter of time before there will be a recognition of this. It is in the present stage an unconscious reaction to that which is behind you so that you feel this rejection and do not understand what it means. They do not either. It is very, very difficult for you to make contacts because of this. It is not personality conflicts. It is the backing which you carry with you at all times which causes the reaction. The reaction of some in your group is based on this. They are not consciously aware of it. It makes it very difficult for all disciples working in the world today to meet this opposition at every hand and yet there is going to come a period of time when this opposition can no longer be suppressed. It will come into the consciousness of man and thus he will begin to seek that which you have behind you, backing you.

You are strong personalities and can take any amount of impact from others. The point is that you need not be so dismayed by it when it is understood by you. The course that the work is taking or the direction that it is taking is an indication of where you stand. The contacts you are making are beginning to be felt in those areas where the most work can be done and this also can be of comfort to you. The areas into which you are reaching and receiving, actually, the most reaction, are those which are the strongest of your contacts. So, there is naturally more reaction in these areas than there are where the impact is not making too much of an impression, or where the purpose behind the others is not so strong. You do not receive as violent a reaction from them because they do not respond to the backing as much as the others where there is a tremendous reaction. Those with the most reaction naturally are the ones who carry the greatest amount of power behind them.

Chapter 24

Right Relationship

An Appearance of Negativity,

Receive and Properly Distribute Energy,

The Relationship of Brotherhood,

A Study Group

One good point to consider is the fact that anything a personality can recognize outside of itself is an outpicturing of that within. I remind you that it is only through application that any concept of truth becomes a fact on the plane in which you are now living. If you can go one step further and in the place of the word application, use precipitation, the problems which you meet and which you overcome at this particular point will not again give you difficulty.

I shall ask you, then, to give your attention to the concept of precipitation as it applies to the goal of the group.

I wish to remind you that as the conditions manifest, if you will first of all realize that you are a group in training, and as such you will meet consciously with those situations which will provide you to adequately pass through this training period.

The problem of relationship, for instance, is one which is predominant in every group which is attempting to be of service to mankind; therefore, it has to be dealt with.

The Disciple and Economy

When next an appearance of negativity manifests within the life and affairs of the group, realize it as constituting a major lesson and meet it as such. Detach from it as personalities since it is not a personality problem. In this manner, you will be able to work more easily as a group and you will be able to pass more quickly from one problem to another until you become adept in this technique. The first mistake is failure to recognize the condition as a world condition. After the major reactions become quiescent, realize that as the members of the group are able to pull together, the first lesson in this period of training will be met and successfully passed.

I am going to be very frank and bring into discussion a problem which is not only trying for small groups of people, but one which is world wide, which is the cause of the major difficulty within the human family today.

This particular problem is one which is shared by all members of a group. That is, to receive and properly distribute energy. Its manifestation is simply wrong relationship. The inability of the individuals to establish with one another the relationship of brotherhood. If anyone in the world has a reason for establishing brotherhood, it is a group of disciples who are dedicated to a common purpose, to recognize the Christ within each other and because of that recognition, to overlook the faults of the personality. They are superficial, they have been acquired in the past due to a lack of understanding. They are eliminated gradually as that understanding is attained. In the meantime these disciples, each one with his own personal habits, his own mannerisms, which are very often a source of irritation, has to meet and to learn to work in service with others. One of the easiest ways to establish right relationship is to realize that when another irritates you because of a personality trait or habit which he has acquired, you in turn are a source of irritation to others, for it is something which no disciple can be free from until he achieves Mastery, and none of you are as yet Masters.

Speaking on a level which you understand, I will tell you the fate of the human family lies in the hands of groups such as this.

If those who grasp The Plan are unable to overcome limitations, or manifest right relationship in order to carry out this work, then how can the human family be expected to live in peace. Very few individuals in the world today have the understanding, and the opportunity which comes with that understanding, which you have.

I am asking you at this time to dispense with your criticism, your dislikes, and resentments, to recognize one another as brothers and work for the common good of mankind.

For the benefit of those unaware of certain manifestations which result in wrong relationships, I shall explain. The group cannot work or study, since the energies which are being poured into the group have not been consciously directed by each member into activity. Study is a service. In a study group disciples are usually on the personality level most of the time. Energy collects in the group astral body, and manifests in focal points in the group as wrong relationship.

Much time and effort is being concentrated on this movement by many with whom you are not acquainted. Because each has made a dedication and responded to the call of service, I am asking you now to establish the relationship which will make it possible to establish right relationship in this area.

Because there manifests a great deal of feeling, no one is responsible for what happens. Each member shares the responsibility for what happens. It is a group condition, not an individual one. It focalizes through certain members of the group, but their responsibility is neither less nor greater. The major cause of this manifestation is a lack (in the group state of consciousness) of service, lack of realization of the Soul. It is this lack which is the major cause of the condition.

Truth sees above and beyond all of the illusions, falsity of the personality. In your reaction there is not a demonstration of truth. That is the one thing you need to face and no one realizes more than I how difficult that is. The most difficult thing to realize is the acceptance of that which one person sees for himself as truth, that for you it may not be. Truth is relative to a man and his consciousness, to a man and his past experience. There is nothing so heart breaking, to speak in terms which each one of you understands, as to see disciples disagree over what they call truth. If you could but release that which you have clutched to yourselves and reach for higher truth which brings all men to one, then you would have found truth.

In a study group each member acts as a personality, each member is trying to take the spotlight to show how much knowledge he has acquired. The entire group is wrong. Therefore, the discussion of the group has not been on the level which would have resulted in enlightenment. The question now is whether or not you are able to meet together as disciples to carry out The Plan to humanity which you are dedicated to serve. When you have arrived at this decision, it only remains for you to carry it out.

Chapter 25

Right Relationship – First Ray

Establishing and Maintaining Stability,
Directing Energies Into Manifestation,
When Someone is Having Difficulty

Because the group has come so far in realization and in application, I am going to take this opportunity to help you with the problem which has heretofore been left for you to struggle with alone. Up to and until this particular time, it has been impossible for us to intervene in any way to aid during this cyclic period of difficulty. I am speaking now of the problem of relationship which is the major problem of the group, and which has again come into cyclic manifestation. As you realize in part, this particular problem is characteristic of a First Ray personality as well as a First Ray group. It is a problem of energies as they come into manifestation on astral levels. It is a problem which is shared not only by all disciples, but by the entire human family, because of the place in evolution which has been reached by the human entity.

As the cyclic period of manifestation of this particular problem makes its appearance, it is felt first and primarily by any and all individuals acting as members of a group. The resident group is the first to receive and channel into the etheric network incoming energies from higher sources. They are also a magnetic pole of attraction for energies circulating within the etheric network of the system, which means that they receive the impact both from above, insofar as vibratory frequency is concerned, and from below. Theirs then, is a particularly difficult task in establishing and maintaining stability at all times, regardless of manifesting conditions. Much of the larger group manifestation of this particular difficulty would be eliminated by this central nucleus if they were capable of receiving and directing these energies into manifestation free from qualifying reactions. Please understand that I am not in any way reprimanding any member of this group.

In considering this problem, each one of you has been given a tremendous volume of words which constitutes in their entirety complete and adequate information and illumination. You pass too lightly over the word which is projected to you with the intent to illumine. I am not, therefore, going to take up your time or my time in projecting that which will only be a repetition of what has already been said. Refer back, each one of you, to all that I have said regarding this problem of relationship; refer back in your minds to the concepts which have been projected. Orient your own thinking in one direction. It is important.

I will add one concept to that which has already been projected. It should not be necessary, however, since it is I shall project it. The difficulty which has been manifesting on physical levels and on astral levels has grown out of proportion. It has been magnified as a result of individual reactions to the difficulties of various persons within the group.

If you will each stop for just a moment and realize that when one individual or one member of the group is having difficulty he should not become the brunt of your criticism, of your reaction. He should receive your love, your understanding and your honest effort to be of help. When one member of the group is manifesting negative reaction, let his brothers rally with a desire to help.

Chapter 25

This is most important, regardless of the type, quality and strength of the manifesting reaction. If this could be done at all times, the individual would very quickly find his footing, would be able to walk out of his own negativity.

Because the group has reached a place where tremendous possibilities of service lie immediately ahead of you, I am making this plea. It may not always be possible for an individual to remain free from reactions; there are many contributing factors to the reaction, but it is possible as a result of the protection which we offer you, for the major part of the group to remain free from negative reaction at any given time. The individual who is having difficulty will vary from time to time, but to place the blame upon that individual, to think or say that he or she is pulling the rest of the group down is wrong; it is justification; it is an alibi, and in this you are failing to recognize a way in which you can be of very great service. I would have you think on this.

The Disciple and Economy

Chapter 26

Right Relationship – Transmutation

Focus any Problem,

Grasp the Dark Forces,

Release the Light

You, as disciples, are given ways and means of handling your personality reactions. The reactions will become increasingly evident as group integration takes place. The demonstration of these truths is the hardest part for the personality to "stomach", for at times you must proceed on blind faith to its ultimate conclusion.

Please proceed with group integration for that is the true power and source of balancing karma in relationship between individuals and between the individual and his subconscious blocks.

In the meantime, focus any problem which you feel you have in direct alignment with the Soul. Move into that magnetic field of the group Soul within your cave in the center of the head. You have the power of the group at your disposal. Grasp the dark forces within you by deliberately bringing the problem up into the cave, drawing its intent out of the subconscious. Bring it out of the muck and bring its related problems with it up into the ajna center where it can be looked at, acted out, mentally accepted as a problem; then bring it into the light of the Soul in the cave. Becoming the third party, the observer, deliberately act out the play. This is always a relationship so there will be two or more in your play.

The Disciple and Economy

You become the audience, watching the actors perform. First you take the part of first one and then another of those actors. You become the person or problem involved, taking on the reactions of each, speaking to each, hitting if the play calls for it, screaming or crying, whatever is necessary to feel the emotion of the experience toward the working out of the play to its ultimate conclusion.

See to it, my brothers, for the longer you hold back from looking at Truth, the longer you are held a prisoner within the form.

Turn on the floodlights at the end of the play. Bathe the stage in Christ's healing light. Have a curtain call for all of the performers, knowing that each has played his part well.

Release the light into the mental body by moving back out to the ajna center. Look at it, knowing that Truth will set you free. You can even be the editor, writing your reactions to the play.

Move into the heart center and Love the situation, letting it go back into the subconscious as Truth.

If another block is inter-related with this one, you know what to do — flood it with the Soul's light using the group magnetic field for the power to rise above the emotion. Take a good hard look at it emotionally and mentally. Flood it with the radiance of the Christ and Love the experience for it has given you an insight into race mind consciousness and you have helped solve humanity's problem through relieving your own. You have helped relieve the congestion within the emotional and mental body of the race through this service to yourself and to your group of brothers.

You have utilized:

Chapter 26

First Ray Will, to deliberately move the problem up into the light.

Second Ray Love of the Soul, to use the light of the Soul and group magnetic field to surround the play in its ring-pass-not alignment with Truth.

Third Ray of Active Intelligence, to analyze the play and draw from it its purpose.

Fourth Ray of Harmony through Conflict, acting out the various parts and emotions of the actors.

Fifth Ray of Concrete Knowledge and Science, looking at the results and absorbing the essence back into the subconscious in its true light.

Sixth Ray of Devotion to an Ideal, that the Soul has manifested a healing and that each inter-related particle will be affected with Christ Light.

Seventh Ray of Ceremonial Magic. This whole act was a ceremony from the opening to the closing curtain, the applause and the floodlights. Your response was your enlightenment and the establishment of Divine Law and Order in your life and affairs.

The Disciple and Economy

Chapter 27

World Group – New Age

Increase the Quantity and Quality of Energy;

Conflict Between Old and New;

Ideal, Vision, and Plan;

Breaking the Barrier

Between the Astral and the Physical

The Mahachohan/Lucille:

The message I am projecting is not confined to any group or individuals, but is one which is being given to all members of the World Group. Therefore, I would suggest that while this is not in the nature of the World Group meeting and while I am speaking directly to only a few of you at this particular time I would ask that the message be recorded and made available to all in the category of world disciples insofar as your spheres of influence are concerned.

The difficulty which all disciples are undergoing at this particular time is based largely on their inability to recognize and work with world conditions. The problems with which they are confronted are interpreted as individual problems, confined to their personal life and affairs, or to their particular group life and its affairs. This limits the disciple's thinking in such a way as to make it impossible for him to grasp the larger world issues and to apply that which is necessary to right those conditions. For that reason, we find disciples failing to integrate their separate fields of knowledge and understanding, and because of that failure they are unable to provide for humanity available answers and solutions to world questions and conditions. Realize first, and let the realization be so complete, so that it is not necessary to be reminded again, that it is utterly impossible for you to know a personal problem. Learn to think in terms of world need and world fulfillment. When you as individuals are confronted with apparent individual problems, relate them to world conditions which are causing the difficulty and work from above downward.

One of these world conditions is the conflict which is produced by the increase of both quantity and quality of new energy which is coming into incarnation at this particular time. I speak anent the Seventh Ray, the coming in of this ray and the passing out of the Sixth Ray. This is creating a conflict, which, as it comes into physical manifestation, results in constant irritation. Remember that as this ray begins to dominate the Sixth Ray, the new forms which are qualified to carry the new teaching, the new culture, the new civilization, are brought into appearance. Until those forms have gained sufficient stabilization, there will be the appearance of conflict between the old and the new.

This age into which the world is passing is characterized by fire. It is the age in which the mind plays the predominant part. As the ray which signifies Divine Law and Order begins to dominate race mind consciousness, the conflict between the astral and the mental consciousness increases in its intensity. Consider the conditions which result when great quantities of fire and water are brought together. I speak symbolically, yes, but the miasma which results is just as real as the fog which sweeps in from the ocean.

Chapter 27

What is not rightly interpreted or realized by disciples is that regardless of the conflict, the objective is one and the same. The ideal for which the astral consciousness and the mental consciousness battle does not change character, is not different today than it was yesterday, is no different in this age than it was in the last age. This is an extremely difficult concept because within the consciousness of each disciple is the condition which we find within the consciousness of the race – the conflict between the mind and the emotions – the ideal on the emotional level which has been sensed by aspirant and disciple down through the ages and the vision on the mental plane – The Plan itself is one and the same. It is necessary to relate the two. One cannot be cast out that the other might live, for each is but an aspect of one reality. They must be brought together and reincarnated in the new form – a form which is capable of carrying both aspects instead of one, a form that is capable of manifesting a small degree of greater perfection than the one which is passing. Every concept, every ideology in the world today is being put to this test. Every activity is put to this same test. Every form, whether that be the physical form of some disciple or the activity which anyone is utilizing to carry out its purpose, every form which does not stand up to this test, every form which cannot carry the dual concept, will pass from existence and the passing will be noted as part of a great struggle.

It is necessary, then, for disciples to recognize this condition as it exists and through methods which are best suited to each one, to make the decisions as they are faced to bring in the New Age. Any activity in which you are engaged which does not carry the energy, which cannot carry the consciousness, must be eliminated. The disciple must be fearless. His must be the ability to discriminate between that which is a part of the new way of life and that which is on its way out. Any form which cannot be seen to be passing must nevertheless

The Disciple and Economy

be released in love. For to hold that form to you is to render yourself inefficient and without use, to put it very bluntly. Do not hold to those old forms. Do not fear that which is new, but become acquainted with the new forms, with the new activity. As you put them into manifestation, do not fear the conflict which they create, but realize that the conflict is the passing of those old outmoded thought-forms which have been giving the race so much trouble for so long a period of time.

That these new forms may appear strange, may be difficult to become adjusted to is true, but only because of your own crystallization. Remember that one of the first things to pass from this age are the old concepts of right and wrong, of good and bad, and as they pass they take with them the forms in which they manifested. Those states of consciousness which are unable to survive without the old forms will disintegrate until a period is again provided for their growth. As those states of consciousness increase, as the result of the passing of the many forms of activity, the disintegration upon the planet will appear great. But the disciple who observes this disintegration knows it for what it is — that it is impossible to build a new building where an old one is standing — and in calm acceptance the disciple proceeds with his construction.

Do not concern yourselves at this time with the form aspect, with what to do when certain things occur. You are seeking old forms and there are none available. Do not plan, but accept that which comes and work as intuitively guided as the work is needed. You are facing conflict, yes, but I would remind you once again that within every storm there is a center of equilibrium. Establish your own center and from there work. Be not dismayed by what you see. When this conflict touches you, when it seems that you are thrown into the very midst of it, accept that of the passing from your life and affairs of the old forms which are no longer of benefit to you. Release them and look to the light with joy.

Once again, it is impossible for you to know a personal problem. You cannot isolate any apparent problem as your own, for there are many, many, many individuals who share in that problem with you. It is a world condition, work with it as such. Outer appearances are not important because none of you are capable of interpreting them.

One of the conditions which is in existence today and which will be increasingly so, is the breaking, in one sense, of the barrier between the astral and the physical planes. That barrier is on its way out. Humanity is orienting itself to an entirely new set of conditions. The astral consciousness is being integrated with the physical plane consciousness and is taking physical incarnation. This is preceded by the emergence of those conditions which were heretofore manifested only on the astral plane. This is the greatest reason for the increased sensitivity and the ability to interpret that which is sensed. You are quickly passing into a period when even time itself must be reoriented. A new set of coordinates must be established in order that the consciousness can manifest Divine Law and Order. Until those coordinates are established, there will be the appearance of chaos in every form which can be imagined.

Any individual whose physical instrument is composed largely of substance which is dominated by the Seventh Ray is responding to this much more rapidly than are others. For it is the Seventh Ray that is bringing in the new age. Anything that comes into manifestation takes the path of least resistance, so that the Seventh Ray form is always, in this particular crisis, the first to manifest that which is new. Where there is no understanding, the manifestation is apparent chaos, until there have been new coordinates established and the proper reorientation of the consciousness to that which is happening.

The very energies which are poured through the Seventh Ray physical instrument increase this condition, so that it would be impossible for the individual, whether he be a disciple, an aspirant, a probationer, or a lesser evolved, to escape the manifesting conditions; he must learn to work with and through them.

Almost all disciples who are in incarnation at this time and who are working with the coming in of the New Age, work through Seventh Ray physical instruments. While this may appear to be difficult, it is fortunate that they do work through Seventh Ray instruments.

In most instances where a physical form is predominantly Sixth Ray, it will pass, since it has been constructed and conditioned by the Sixth Ray for the purpose of carrying the consciousness of and bringing into manifestation the ideals of the passing age. It is no longer of any use. There are some instances, in the cases of disciples who function through Sixth Ray instruments, where the old form will not pass, but will shift from the Sixth to another ray. This, however, will be rare, since it is much easier to do away with the old forms and construct new ones, than it is to recondition that which is old. In an instance of a shift from the Sixth Ray to the Seventh Ray, the instrument will be well conditioned by the Seventh Ray. It will be impossible to eliminate the Sixth Ray entirely, since a certain amount of Sixth Ray is needed to carry out to completion the work of the passing age. There must be a survival of that which can be considered perfection in the passing age so that the new civilization can be brought in on a higher level, rather than going back and building again on the same level. Much out of this present age – the age which is passing, will survive. The teaching of the Christ which was presented at the beginning of this age, will not only survive, but will come into its

232

Chapter 27

full manifestation during the next age. There are, therefore, some disciples who must carry a certain amount of
Sixth Ray. Actually, what takes place with these particular disciples is not so much a shift from one ray to
another, as it is a carrying of aspects of one ray and
aspects of another.

The Disciple and Economy

Chapter 28

World Group Cycle

Cycles in the Evolution of Consciousness, Divine Discrimination, Concrete Mind Power, Vast Body of Light

My purpose in speaking with you is to bring to each and every one of you a realization of the need which is present in the world today and the way in which you both individually and collectively, can help to fulfill that need.

Most of you are aware of the state of confusion in which the human consciousness finds itself. Most of you are aware of the cause of that condition, realizing that it is a cyclic period of opportunity which can be seized and utilized for the betterment of the race. These cycles appear often in the evolution of consciousness; however, seldom are they as significant and as important as the one in which we find ourselves today.

In the past, it has always been possible for an individual to seize such an opportunity and through the strength of his mind, his devotion and his understanding, swing the human race onto the right path, taking the next step in evolutionary progress. Today, such a thing is not possible. No one individual can seize this opportunity and by himself take the lead in the salvation of the race, for this cyclic period offers the opportunity for the human race to enter into a new state of consciousness, for every individual to realize himself as a Soul and as such to function in cooperation with his brothers.

All of you know, if you will think back, of the great influence which Jesus the Christ was able to bring to bear upon the human consciousness and how long that influence has lasted. I would ask you to consider how great the opportunity is, when not one individual, but many thousands can, if they so choose, attain to this state of consciousness; can bring the perfection which is within every man, into outer manifestation. Most of you have heard many times, references made to the World Group of disciples, but few of you have realized the actual fact of such a group. Few of you have realized that not only does such a group exist but that any individual who chooses to cooperate with the forces of light is a part of that group.

The purpose of the teaching which you have received is to bring each one of you a realization of the existence of such a group and the opportunity to serve as one of its members, under the Christ. The goal of this work is the externalization, on the physical plane, of a group of disciples, living in all parts of the world who are so at-one in purpose that they can, when given the word, unite and invoke the aid of the Christ, to the needs of humanity.

One of the very great difficulties presented in the formation of such a group is present in every small group. Those who are separated on the physical plane establish a rapport which supersedes time and space and their work is very effective, but when brought together as personalities in mental, emotional and physical instruments, the friction which results renders the work ineffective. The need today is for the bringing together on the plane of the personality of these disciples and their ability to rise above personality friction; to become so one-pointed in purpose that the personality can be

Chapter 28

utilized as an instrument of service in the world in which they live.

Many times, I have told some of you that that which you see in another, that causes undesirable reactions, is but an out-picturing from within yourself, or you would not be capable of recognizing it. I am making a plea. I am asking that those of you who sincerely desire to serve, those who have made dedications, cease the criticism; it is destructive. Realize that you are brothers in purpose, that anything else is unimportant and unite to work for one thing, the illumination of mankind.

Criticism is always the result of a lack of understanding. Where there is understanding there cannot be criticism. Very often words which are idly spoken do not carry a great deal of critical thought behind them, nonetheless they evoke critical thought, for they are one source of misunderstanding. That includes a love for everyone. Not only a love which is projected to those whom you meet, but love which goes out with thought and therefore has its effect upon many whom you never meet in the physical instrument.

There is one other point I would like to bring up at this time. When I speak of non-criticism I also include critical thoughts and feelings which you direct to yourselves: apparent failure to rise to an occasion, a blunder, a mistake, that we must see as clearly within ourselves as we do within others. Realize that as you establish greater contact with the Soul, you are going to bring down into the threefold instrument illumination, the light of the Soul which reveals, and as it enters each one of the three instruments, it will reveal that which is within — the undesirable as well as the desirable. Then when you see some part of yourself which you do not like, realize that it is an indication of progress; it is illumination and go on from there. Do not fall into the habit of depression as a result of illumination. Learn to laugh at yourself once in awhile and not to take yourself too seriously, certainly not the instruments.

One must have reached a state of consciousness which is characterized by Divine Discrimination before he is capable of constructive criticism. Actually the terminology is very poor. When asked a direct question by a brother, it is right to answer him truthfully. If the motive is love and service, then the action which results will be right action. But there are few individuals whose motive is such that they are selfless, particularly in the area of another's lack of understanding.

I am going to talk to you regarding the reason that this particular effort toward integration is being made at this time. You have reached the place where, due to your own rapidly developing sensitivity and the added strain of world conditions, it is going to be necessary that great effort, one-pointedness of purpose and goal be made to carry you, as a group, through the coming months. Remember you are blazing a trail for others to follow.

I am going to point out to you the two outstanding qualities within a group. One of the major difficulties is that there is a great concrete mind power available within a group, and when rightly utilized will make it possible for the group to play a very important part in constructing the forms which will bring in the New Age. My brothers, that very strength of concrete mind available as a group, makes it difficult for the group to rise above that level in times of stress, to function as a service unit.

Your second greatest strength is in the purity of your motive and your ability to sacrifice personal attainment to group service activities. For that, my brothers, we who watch and teach are very grateful, and it is this quality which has carried you through thus far, through

Chapter 28

the many karmic adjustments and personality conflicts attendant to group work and integration.

It is not with any feeling of doubt that we speak with you, there is no doubt that there will be the desired progress made. There is one point that is important to remember, in this type of a group, and that is the tendency to learn, to acquire new knowledge. This tendency will not be overcome by an individual or a group, without a parallel progress of intuitional development. I am going to ask that you not attempt, because of your ability to intellectually assimilate material, to jeopardize expansion of group consciousness by too rapid a study of this lesson material. In a very short time, because of your increasing sensitivity, it will be possible for each and every one of you to see and know what is meant by embodiment of concepts. The thorough embodiment of concepts projected is particularly important to those group members engaged in subjective and healing activities.

The demand by disciples all over the world is for specific instructions and methods as to how to work more effectively in subjective and healing activities. Instruction and methods, other than that which you are receiving would be useless to you, for only as you embody and put into manifestation – build into your instruments the concepts contained in the lesson material – will you be able to work more effectively, to use specific instructions, and my brothers, they will not be necessary when you cease intellectual seeking.

That does not mean that the work you are doing now is not effective, for any method which you use is effective and that effectiveness is determined by the purity of your motive. I ask that you cease concern over the results of the work you are doing. It is very powerful and will become increasingly so as the group becomes more one-pointed in purpose and merges with other groups working in other areas.

Disciples of a certain degree in the World Group have attained illumination upon certain subjects, particularly that of personality integration and control of the astral body, which will have a stabilizing influence on all other disciples functioning in this world body. While those disciples are removed from you as far as distance is concerned, and you are not personally associated with them, they are members of the vast body of light of which you are also members. Their increased illumination will aid every disciple who stands below them, or let us say every disciple who follows them on this path of discipleship.

I would suggest that you reach out during the coming months to this stabilizing influence. Reach out to these realizations which have been attained and projected in your direction, not as individuals but as levels of consciousness. If you can do this consciously, you will benefit greatly and your ability to serve will be strengthened.

I would suggest also that you include this relationship which does exist in all disciples by thinking toward them with love and with gratitude, for they have in the midst of difficult daily experience, established in their lives a materialized form of truth which is of tremendous service to every disciple working in the field. Do not concern yourselves with the identity of these disciples, they are unknown to you and will remain unknown insofar as the plane of the personality is concerned.

Chapter 29

World Group Meeting

The World Condition,
Piercing the Barrier Between the Planes,
The Downpour of First Ray

A meeting of the World Group was called as a result of a manifestation of the world condition which has actually precipitated a rather important crisis in the present evolutionary development of the human race. While you were not as yet ready as a group to actually take part in this meeting, certain aspects of it, certain information and instruction which you can, if you so choose, utilize both as clarification and as a type of service activity is being passed on to you.

I shall very briefly explain the world condition referred to and the nature of the crisis which has developed.

The manifesting condition is a type of negativity which when viewed from the perspective which is able to look into or see that which is taking place in various parts of the world and properly relate those happenings, is of grave concern to those of Us who are attempting to guide the affairs of the world into what I shall call a point of stabilization as it manifests in the life of the individual. It may seem to the incarnating consciousness as of little importance and having little effect.

However, when it is seen as a general world condition

manifesting in all levels of consciousness in all walks of life and among all nationalities, it becomes a problem of planetary significance.

All of you have been more or less aware of this condition individually. Some few of you have been aware of it as a group condition, but only the Hierarchy has been able to see this particular manifestation as it really is.

I am going to go back and attempt to bring to you a realization of the primary cause of the increased attention which is being given the training of all disciples by the Hierarchy. Quite some time ago it was known that humanity was approaching a crisis, and that the mass of humanity would be faced with a decision as to the path of experience which would be initiated and carried out to cover an approximate period of 2000 years. It could also be seen that as this crisis approached there would be manifestations of a kind of negativity extremely difficult to meet and overcome.

These manifestations have been interpreted by many different organizations, many occult groups, as every kind of destruction – war, cataclysms, etc. The exact nature of the manifesting condition could not be known until it actually approached appearance. It was known, however, there would be certain very definite manifestations. An intensive period of training, more intensive than you can possibly realize was put before all aspirants and disciples incarnate. The type and life they have been forced to experience, that has been the essential training. The entry into some kind of occult or mental training according to the consciousness conceived has been another aspect of that training. One of the known manifestations for which these individuals have been and are still being trained was the breaking or piercing of the vibratory barrier between astral and physical planes. This particular manifestation is well under way and is primarily at this particular time the cause of the world condition to which I earlier referred. This is difficult for you to understand and possibly for you to grasp. It is extremely difficult to discuss with you because of limitations of your consciousness.

The effect of the nearness of the astral to the physical plane is the increase of astral energy which disciples are now experiencing. Certain world thought-forms which carry great emotional impact are very close to breaking through that barrier and making an appearance on the physical world. Their nearness is actually activating the solar plexus center and emotional nature. It will not be in the too distant future when these thought-forms will be visible and various aspects in the astral plane will not only be visible but will impinge on the awareness of the brain consciousness.

In addition to this manifestation, there is a downpour of First Ray energy into the etheric network of the human family. I would have you consider first what is the major activity of the First Ray, not when viewed from the vantage point of the disciple but viewed from the vantage point of the ray itself and its intended purpose and the manner that purpose is experienced in the world of appearance. The world of the First Ray is extraction from form. Its impression in the world is that of the destroyer. It is First Ray which predominates in transition from the physical instrument to more subtle planes (known as death). This energy always predominates during the finish of any age or cycle of manifestation. Its concentrated projection results in dissolution of form. The old form still in the instrument at the end of any age is a hindrance to the coming in of the new, and is disintegrated through activity of the First Ray.

Pouring in with almost equal proportion is the Fifth Ray (advancing science) and all thought of concrete nature (not crystallization but of progress) as well as Seventh Ray. The reception of First Ray by the disciple, to say nothing of humanity, is creating much havoc due to wrong interpretation and qualification of the energy. The disciple is not qualified to work with First Ray alone, not equipped to use First Ray except through love. In order to balance these three ray energies as they make their impact on your consciousness and in order to direct, there must be a concentration on love.

In order to meet the condition which is manifesting on the astral plane the disciple must depersonalize the condition he is experiencing. Your greatest problem is the fact that you are meeting something you are not able to see as a part of yourself. If you were in the midst of disaster, war on the physical plane, etc., you would meet these conditions perfectly. This condition is much greater than any type of disaster which you might be called upon to face and it calls for just as great a degree of selflessness as would disaster. If you were to meet with the manifestation on the physical plane, you would forget yourself in service, as you attempt to alleviate the pain and suffering of the masses around you. You have not been able to meet the need of the present time. You have not seen this as a world need. Disassociate from it. This is true of all disciples who are working to serve humanity during this period. Any prediction of impending crisis, chaos, confusion, etc., is, my brother, in manifestation and it is demoralizing the race. All disciples are being called upon now to attempt to rise above their own difficulties, their own emotions, to meet this manifesting condition. Please try to do two things:

1. To become receptive to that Love which is the attribute of the Christ, which can pour through each one as channels.

2. To recognize your own emotional disturbances as indicative of service. Imagine your disturbance increased by sharing with 100 people, let alone the entire race, and you will see the picture.

Chapter 29

Work as you would if the manifestation were a war into which you as individuals have been plunged.

Eventually there will be an integration between astral and physical planes where astral will be as visible as the physical. However, this will not happen without a great deal of various kinds of manifestation prior to the actual rupture of the barrier. There have been instances when that barrier has been so thin that the barrier was visible momentarily. This will increase, will happen many times. The influence of the astral plane is what disciples must work with at this time and it will become increasingly great.

As these thought-forms near the physical plane (it is extremely difficult to define the emotion, it will be mixed) they will take many varying manifestations: Direct impact on solar plexus and from there to the brain. There are subconscious reactions to it. Do not confuse emotional disturbances with therapy.

Go easy on meditation; concentrate attention on love; act as channels for Divine Love. Attempt to attain meditative state at all times. Concentrate on Love, radiating center of Christ light.

The Disciple and Economy

Chapter 30

Right Relationship with
the World Group of Disciples

A New Effort on Behalf of Humanity,
The New Civilization, The New Methodology,
The Point of Transition

Later you will find yourselves within a World Group. Only when you become group conscious within your own group relationships, only then will you be permitted to find yourselves within the World Group because the World Group is not composed of individuals. The World Group is the One Life which is constituted of all group units, the disciples in the world who function within their own particular Ashramic units. These constitute the World Group, and you find your relationship within the larger group only after you have become group conscious in your own unit and entered into an integrated group life as such. Then you enter into the World Group and find your function.

I would like to stress, because there is much glamour here regarding this concept of group, the tendency, and it is natural, of the individual disciple to find his place within the vast group of disciples in the world without realizing that no individual disciple finds himself in the World Group. The World Group is not constructed of individual disciples. It is constructed of groups.

When this group has become a one life and every member

within it is group conscious, then this group will find its right relationship, its place within the World Group. For instance, take all the Ashrams within the Hierarchy. These Ashrams constitute in their sum total a vast group life. But each finds his place within it via his own group life, his particular vehicle in the group sense. Each Ashram is a group life.

The recognition that some of you have made regarding certain individuals as being a member of the World Group of Disciples who have carried the responsibility of the manifestation of The Divine Plan for humanity for many ages in the past is absolutely correct. Also the recognition, the realization that a relationship must be made with these disciples, this is true. But much more than that – the group, while it can and must recognize its own capacity, its own particular potential, its own note, so to speak, must also be able to recognize the value, the place in the scheme of things, of each particular note which is predominant within the World Group as it stands today, but also the note of others with whom you will come in contact. Do not become so ingrown as a group that you become critical as regards all other groups.

I am going to explain something to you that is of primary importance to you from this moment on. You will find very few of your kind in incarnation outside of this group. I would suggest that you take this into consideration. You are a group of souls in incarnation; those in the world who are of your particular kind, will be attracted to you as group members. As a group you have a service to perform, to render, a contribution to make to the evolutionary growth and development of humanity. But at the same time, you are young; you constitute a new effort on behalf of humanity, and you have to earn your value. You will find that the successful manifestation of your service activity as you proceed along its natural path, will result as you establish right relationship as a service group within the World Group of Disciples. You have then to be accepted by them, regardless of your newness and your strangeness; they are in control. This is correct. They are in charge; they have been in charge and for the most part their path has been that of the mystic. So that as you are able to successfully establish a right relationship with them, work with them in consciousness, then in instrumentality, you will find their cooperation opening the doors for you. This is extremely important. You ask how this relationship can be made. Your meditation is primarily in preparation to this task or assignment. Because, in order to establish right relationship with these disciples, you are going to have to learn how to meet them on their level with the energies they can recognize. Just because they are disciples, you cannot expect them to be educated in your way; you are coming after them. And as all phases of evolutionary plan overlap, there is an overlapping here in a sense. You are the children taking over the reins of the civilization from the parents who are going out of, leaving that civilization. These disciples who have held these reins and who have served The Divine Plan for humanity for many, many, many incarnations, will not be coming back in during this next age to serve as disciples; they are not coming in. A new group is coming in, following after them.

It is difficult always for the younger generation to understand the older generation, and I am speaking in the soul sense. Do not think that you are more highly evolved than they, because your ways are different, because you are not. And as it is difficult always for the younger generation to understand the older, and in some ways for the older to understand the younger; you must understand that the misunderstanding which these disciples have of you will disappear as they leave the limitations of their service pattern. But do not forget that while they realize that a new dispensation is coming in, and while they realize that a new group is

The Disciple and Economy

taking over where they are leaving off, they are much concerned about the ability, the capacity of these new groups; and I am not referring to you now as individuals but to the Ashram as a whole.

They are much concerned about the ability of these young upstarts, so to speak, to take the job and to carry it out.

There is one other thought I wish to bring out here, in relationship to this. Remember that the civilization out of which humanity is passing has been the Third Ray nature which dealt with the building of forms – many, many, many forms. Now the new civilization into which humanity is entering is that of the Seventh Ray nature which has to do with the right use of forms: the ceremony of spirit within matter.

A disciple during the old civilization, during this past age, has had to build many forms in order to serve humanity; in order to take the path of least resistance to the human consciousness. These forms which are so abhorrent to your state of consciousness were absolutely necessary for the service of humanity and they were constructed by that group of disciples – and I refer now to all of the Ashrams – under the Mahachohan of the past period – and I am referring now to a much longer time than 2500 years, as the forms through which the disciple could serve humanity.

Now, today you are coming in – you along with many others – in the new Ashram, with a new method, new techniques, which have no use for most of the old forms which were constructed out of the energy of the Third Ray. Peace has to somehow be made between the old and the new. And you realize it, surely, that it is this tremendous conflict of incoming and outgoing energies, actually, within which the consciousness of humanity is imprisoned and caught up, that is primarily the cause

250

of this tremendous crisis of opportunity in which humanity finds itself.

So that at your level as disciples, you find yourselves in the same situation, of course, at your level. Do not make war or enter into war with these whom you find almost an antipathy. Do not do this; make your peace. Accept service which the past has rendered, and help them to find their way out of it, because they are faced with a very serious and severe problem. As souls, on soul levels, that problem is reflected into their consciousness as disciples within the world of affairs. Do not forget that it has been absolutely necessary for them to step down every concept in truth for which they have been made responsible, to step it down to the very lowest level in the astral plane in order to serve. This does not mean that they are disciples who are polarized or focused in the astral. No, it means that they have created a certain kind, a certain type of astral body through which they work in order to reach humanity.

Now you are being trained to serve humanity through the lower concrete mind rather than the astral body. But, before you find yourselves in a position which relates you as the World Group of Disciples with humanity, you are going to have to step down much of that which you have received. You are going to have to be able to relate with humanity via the astral body. Therefore, in your relationship with these disciples, in your consciousness, accept this as necessary. Recognize their discipleship, recognize their value to The Divine Plan; realize that if it were not for them it would be utterly impossible for you to be functioning at all, for it is through their service to you during the past that you have been brought to this point. Therefore, as you meet them, regardless of how you may be repelled by some of the expressions which you do not understand, regardless of this, accept their discipleship as that love which you know for one another. Do not be selfish with it.

The Disciple and Economy

Bring it down and give it expression; feel it in relationship to these others. Feel it because if you can do this, you will find that they will find it much easier to accept you and your ways, which are so different from theirs. And I would tell you that among themselves, as disciples, they do practice their beliefs; they do live in their daily life and affairs, concepts to which you are aspiring. They may not call them by the same names, but they do live them; and you have much to learn from them, and in return, much to give.

This group will find it very difficult to move into the service of humanity, into its proper place, until it has learned to establish its right relationship. I must warn you, up to this time you have had very little contact with the World Disciples, but this group on higher Ashramic levels, has been accepted; this technique, this method, which was, to a certain point an experiment, has been accepted by the Hierarchy as the new methodology. Therefore, you are going to be brought into contact with many disciples within the World Group. You will find yourselves being brought into contact with many of them who are old in the physical sense; they are weary. Many of these disciples have been coming in almost constantly in order to carry the burden of world service for humanity; they are weary. Because there is a problem for them in handing over the reins, so to speak, because they are going out and know that they are not returning, you have a great service to render to them. You are going to be brought into contact with them and it is certainly My hope that you will be able to serve them by carrying to them the presence which will assure them that they are not leaving humanity to sink, so to speak. It is extremely important. Do not try to change their ways, do not disagree and argue with them, regarding the forms – these are unimportant – but relate to them with love, with understanding and if they have something to teach you – which they do, believe me – accept that. And now, I do not refer to the forms; I do not refer to the glamours; I am referring to the quality which they do have, which they do embody. Carry then, this presence to them, so that as they do go out, it can be in peace. In other words, give them your peace.

You will find yourselves being brought into contact with some who are in young instruments; they are the point of transition. The responsibility shifts through them, from the old Ashram to the new, from the disciple of the old school to the disciple of the new. So it is also of vital importance that you establish right relationship with them in order not to create pairs of opposites which would result in opposition that would not be good for them, or for you, or for the humanity you both serve. Think on these thoughts and at any time in the future that you are presented with this problem, or when you are considering it, if you wish to invoke answers regarding it, further clarification will be available to you.

The Disciple and Economy

Chapter 31

Divine Intervention – Wesak

The Aspiration of Humanity,
Major Service Contribution,
The Divine Plan is Your Boss

Master John:

There are of course many techniques that are good when you have trouble with your alignment. The best way to improve the alignment is to study. I do not mean practice, but to study the meditation technique so that you grasp it firmly in mind and can visualize the alignments which are established via meditation techniques throughout the entire day. You visualize after having studied the techniques so you can see them clearly. Draw diagrams if you wish; become familiar with them and understand the purpose of each alignment, the frequency into which it moves, etc.; and then visualize in living light, you might say, these alignments which are particularly for you, throughout the entire day. This should be of help for any student, and for anyone who is having difficulty of this kind.

I would speak to you regarding Divine Intervention for it is of major importance to the whole of the group life, and as a group unit. This is not only a great difficulty to you, but it is of major importance, the major import, at this particular time. I am going to explain to you some of the reasons for this condition which you are all feeling to a greater or lesser degree. As you are feeling them, so are all other members of the group life, and I might add, so are most of the disciples working within the body of humanity at this time, feeling these difficulties in one way or another.

You have now entered into the approach to one of the major Wesak Festivals in this century. Much depends on the focus of aspiration achieved by the whole of humanity at the time of this festival; for the degree of focused aspiration will determine the degree of Divine Intervention which can be permitted into the life and affairs of humanity at this particular time. I hope you are following me. In other words, this particular festival is one of the most important in this century, the opportunity presented to both the Hierarchy and humanity insofar as Divine Intervention is concerned, is very great. But of course, such an opportunity is always beset with much opposition. From now until the time of the Wesak, there will be an increasing opposition to the ability of the human entity to focus any aspiration whatsoever. This opposition will strike out at all of humanity, not at any one particular group or any one individual more than any other. It will effect all, will move out, strike out at all, and will be effective to the degree that the individual, whether he be a disciple or an average human being, can be rendered sufficiently unstable to make it impossible for him to focus aspiration.

During a period of this kind there is, of course, always the tremendous effort being made, both through disciples who are functioning within the body of humanity incarnate, and those who are functioning discarnate on astral and mental levels, to invoke aspiration from the consciousness of humanity. This is effective to a very great degree. But on the other hand, oppositional forces will manifest in whatever way will best serve to render the individual incapable of focusing any aspiration whatsoever. It is the aspiration of humanity always, both in total and in groups, which invokes any Divine Intervention, regardless of the form that intervention takes at any particular time.

I cannot tell you what form the intervention will take as a result of this Wesak Festival; it can take many forms, it is not limited to one. But I can tell you that very close to the human family are a number of very highly evolved souls who are preparing to come into incarnation if the invocative appeal of the totality of human consciousness is great enough to render their entry into the arena of human affairs effective, of use and worthwhile. This then would be one of the forms because of the crisis with the world economy, which came into focus some time ago.

We know that the opportunities for Divine Intervention can relate also with the world economy. I will go a little further to recall to your minds, those of you who already know and to those of you who do not, that each year at the time of the Wesak Festival the aspirations of humanity are gathered into a number of foci by different groups of disciples who are consciously working within the body of humanity. Then from within each of these foci, the group lifts further the aspirations of humanity which they have gathered and transmit those aspirations directly, via their own higher alignments, to the overshadowing Christ and to the Buddha, His brother, who stands with Him at this time to release to the waiting humanity that which is the way of Divine Intervention. For instance, of guidance, of higher energies, of grace, of ideas, etc., to release in the way of Divine Intervention that which the aspirations of humanity have invoked into their life and affairs. This takes place during the Full Moon of Taurus each year.

It is difficult sometimes to inspire in humanity as a whole, conscious aspirations. Many are so busy with their daily problems, with their individual, personal life and affairs, that sometimes they forget such things as aspiration. Many deliberately turn away from the idea of anything higher than humanity itself. And yet, on a subconscious level within the body of humanity, there is aspiration — great aspiration. Practically every act into which man enters from so-called self-motivation, wrong motivation insofar as disciples are concerned, is really aspirational in nature even though the individual himself does not realize this. What is it, for instance, that motivates a man to be a better thief than was his father or than is anyone else? It is the tremendous drive, tremendous evolutionary force, which is behind every human being and accompanied by an aspiration to God, even though that aspiration is very often unknown to the individual himself.

The many disciples in the world, according to their degrees of discipleship and their capacity for the work, enter into a very intensive service activity on the approach to this Taurus Full Moon. Their effort is to evoke, call forth from within the consciousness of humanity, conscious aspiration to The Divine Plan, a better way of life, to God. It makes little difference what name is given so long as the consciousness of humanity is aspiring vertically to that which overshadows him. These disciples then, work to evoke this aspiration outward and upward and at the same time the opposition works to render such capacity or ability to aspire impossible. So that anything which can be done to confuse, to bring about emotional disturbance, the precipitation of unpleasant karma, etc., all of this is also happening, and there is quite a battle, one might say, between the light and the dark forces during this period.

One of the major opportunities relating with this particular festival, with this particular Wesak, has to do with the world economy. You realize that the problem of economy insofar as this group is concerned has been very great. We look at this; we face it; we see it. The

Chapter 31

appearance has been one of financial lack, financial imbalance, even restrictions as far as activities are concerned. And it is most indicative that many of the individuals (most of them) who have been attracted into this particular group life, who work within this particular Ashram, are at that state of consciousness within the body of humanity which is particularly representative of this trouble. They are idealistic in nature, not prone to get out in the world and work for money, have great aspiration and dedication to service, have many fears and most definitely, so far, the inability to establish right economic relationship within the world of affairs. This is a problem of a particular state of consciousness, you understand, and while it is a problem of a particular state of consciousness, on a discipleship level, it is one of the major tests of initiation, my brothers. This is difficult to face because for so long the group has worked with this problem. It becomes tired of it, and I do not blame any one of you. It is a tiresome problem that the group has been given, in truth, one of the most important problems you will ever have to face (in this level of discipleship in which you find yourselves). Because once you have solved this problem of economy, you will have solved all of your service problems. Make no mistake about it, once you have mastered the energy, force, and substance of your economy, you will have found the ways and means to put your ideas, your concepts, your vision of The Divine Plan into outer physical manifestation.

Now I realize, more perhaps than do you, that these words are of little solace to you because I'm not telling you how to solve your problems. I am simply showing you it is there, and you do not really need to know it is there, but I just want to show you the nature of it and to give you the understanding why there is no Master, no member of the Hierarchy, who can tell you precisely how to resolve this problem. It is like the child who is given certain problems in arithmetic for homework. If his father does the problems each night for him, he will have gained nothing other than a good grade, you understand, which is false.

It is for you as souls, with the power, the wisdom and the intelligence at your disposal to resolve these problems and in so doing, to take your initiation. It is not easy; I do not envy you. And yet I do not fear for you nor am I overly concerned. The capacity to resolve this problem is yours and because it is a major problem, a part of a station of consciousness peculiar to this group, it will become one of the major service contributions which this group will make within the body of humanity.

That which presents the greatest difficulty always carries the greatest service potential. Yet while the problem is always with you, and always will be, the period between now and the Taurus Full Moon may be more difficult than any other which you have undergone (and I refer now to this group as a whole), and yet it presents the greatest opportunity. Therefore, my suggestion to all of you is to work with it not alone as individuals, for you cannot do this; it is too great a problem for you to work with all by yourself. Work with it from the focus within the group soul life with all of the wisdom, all of the will, and all of the intelligence which is at your command. Regardless of your economy, regardless of your problems and your difficulties, because this is the key to the solution of the problem anyway, make every effort to enter into the service activity of disciples in the world of affairs during this most important cycle, this most important time of the year.

If you in your wonderings as to where and how you are going to get the money to pay the rent, to buy groceries, or to do this or do that, etc., fail to render the service which you are capable of rendering with that economy which is real, that is, with your minds and with your emotions and your physical brains, then you will have failed to put to right use in service to The Plan that economy which is yours to put to use. I refer now not to your dollars, or your lack of dollars, but to your thought life, your emotional life and their focus in and through your brains. If you can link up with all disciples in the world and join them in their effort to evoke aspiration from within the consciousness of humanity (and remember this is the only means of an alignment which the average human being has) to evoke that aspiration at the time of the actual Wesak, bring it into focus within the group life and add to it the aspiration of the group life, lifting it in its frequency and directing it directly to the overshadowing Christ via an invocative appeal for Divine Intervention, if you are able to do this, regardless of outward appearances, regardless of what may be happening in the physical world of economy, then you will have taken a major step forward in the solution of your problems, though I realize it is difficult for you to relate one to the other at this time.

For every moment or day that you become unstable as a result of the outer appearances, to the degree where you cannot detach sufficiently long enough to carry out your meditative, subjective service activity, to this degree do you manifest a continuing lack in your economy. You realize as disciples now you are working with The Divine Plan no matter what is your other activity. The Divine Plan really is your boss, if you would put it that way, and in reality the source of your supply. The laborer is worthy of his hire to the degree of his labor, and that degree is always measured according to his capacity. I would have you think of this because here is where you are now as a group: a whole overall group life.

You understand, time here is not involved but rather potency; the power of your focus whether it is held for a second or an hour. This is the degree, the measure, of the labor of a disciple. It is something for you to think about.

The Disciple and Economy

I do not mean to imply to forget the problem because the problem is not solved by running away from it. No, I do not mean this. What I do mean is that there is certain labor, certain service activity, within which every disciple, due to the very fact of his discipleship, due to his identity as a conscious Soul, is obligated to enter.

It is only natural for the disciple, particularly at a certain degree of discipleship, to forget the importance of the subjective activity which relates to the whole of humanity due to the overwhelming appearance of personal and group problems on the physical plane of affairs. It is easy to forget the other work, and yet the solution or perhaps I should say solutions, to this apparent problem with which he is faced daily in the physical world, lie in his service activities to the One Life within which he lives and moves and has his being.

If one man, or one particular state of consciousness in a group, is desperately ill, another is having all kinds of difficulty in relationships, another may be in prison, another may be facing immediate death, yet this group's greatest difficulty seems to be with economy. If any one of these outer problems is powerful enough in its appearance to pull him down from his focus as a disciple, to render him ineffective, inactive – *inactive*, my brothers – as a Conscious Soul Incarnate, then who has won? The opposition has won, has it not? And, in the winning, will it not use over and over again the same problems because it knows that with these appearances it can conquer the disciple, it can pull him out of his identity as a conscious soul, and it can render him ineffective. If enough disciples throughout the world can be laid low in battle like this, then the forces of light may lack for vehicles.

It does not mean to forget your problems, only to detach from them long enough to establish the strongest, most powerful focus as a Conscious Soul Incarnate of which

Chapter 31

you are capable and direct your attention to the service of humanity away from and apart from your personal problems. You would be amazed to see how many disciples during these kinds of times (and I speak now of the trials, the troubles, the tests of initiation), even though they meditate perhaps one, two or three hours daily, focus their attention on their personal problems. Now, liken this to a soldier on the battlefield who stops in the middle of the battle to think about himself or to write a letter to his wife.

Now this does not mean that the disciple should not meditate in order to resolve his problems; he should. But never should that meditation take away from or impinge upon the service which he renders to humanity, the consciousness of humanity. The meditations for the solution of his personal problems should always be in addition to the service mediation. And if he is just too worn out when the time comes, let him then simply align his problems with The Divine Plan for humanity and ask the Christ to please take care of them for him. Do you see what I am trying to get across to you? You are working, the moment you become a disciple, the moment you make your dedication.

You really sign a contract with The Divine Plan for humanity, you know. This is the organization, you might say, for which you are working. You have said to those who are, if I may put it that way, in charge of the manifestation of The Divine Plan: "Here I am, as a Conscious Soul Incarnate. I like your organization. I think it is better than any other one, and I want to work for it. Will you let me?" And always the organization, those in charge, consult with one another and they say "Yes, you may work, and this is what you can do now, where you are".

What you can do may not seem to be a great deal to you. Perhaps an hour of concentrated and directed thought

The Disciple and Economy

every day, going out and not even creating effects which you are able to see with your own eyes or to hear with your ears may not seem very important. It may seem so unimportant that in the face of what appears to be more important issues, like what am I going to eat for dinner tonight or how will I pay my rent tomorrow, you let it slide so that you can give attention to these other things. Well, you see, The Divine Plan for humanity has its relationship to every state of consciousness, every individual, and every happening, every event within the life and affairs of humanity.

That Divine Plan has its relationship to the economy as well as it does to everything else, and certainly it has its relationship to the economy of the disciple. Do you realize this? If the disciple is going to invoke that relationship into his own economy it must be through the right use of the most important economy he has: his mental energy, his astral force and his etheric substance. So if he puts these to use, if he labors in service to The Divine Plan, then it cannot help but make its relationship to his economy and The Divine Plan of his economy, the economy of the disciple in the world of affairs, and of the group of disciples. *It must manifest.*

But again remember what I said: The laborer is worthy of his hire and always in the degree of his labor. We refer here not to the time spent but to the totality of effort in any one second or any one cycle of effort: the potency, the power, the one-pointedness of the attention he gives to his service. Let this be first, then give your attention to these problems, apply the Wisdom to them and make the effort to work them out. You will find that it will be much easier to do after you have rendered your service to humanity with the activity of The Divine Plan, much easier than it is before you have given that service, because it is the service of the disciple that invokes aid, help, for him.

Chapter 31

Rationalization is a very good word. The area of the mind which perceives form gives interpretation of what it perceives; it slays the real. The real meaning which is there for it to perceive is killed by its interpretation. The mind, you see, depicts. It is not the purpose of the mental body to conceive or to reason. This is a mistake in understanding, and the misuse of the mental body. The mental body depicts, out-pictures. The consciousness then enters into that picture and it perceives what is depicted by the mind. The mind has its particular nature; it is separative. It has to be. How else could it depict; how else could a form be constructed if it were not by a separation of one thing from other things. The consciousness, then, misuses the mind as it identifies with its nature. It takes on that nature; and instead of interpreting that which the mind is depicting, it interprets rather than separates the nature of the mind, so that it does not see the reality. The reality does not come through, and of course this is the last of the matter within which the soul of humanity has been imprisoned and is to be mastered. It is as the mind has depicted in form the Divine Polarity that man has interpreted that polarity as pairs of opposites. And thus the great illusion is created. That illusion is a mental one, as consciousness identifies with its own nature, which is inclusive rather than exclusive, which identifies with and as. This is the nature of consciousness: to identify, to synthesize, to bring everything together into a one. Consciousness identifies with its own nature and then supersedes the nature of the mind, while at the same time using it rightly; then is it enabled to manipulate that mind to create the reality rather than the illusion.

The Disciple and Economy

Chapter 32

Synthesis

The Center of Synthesis for the World,

Channeling Group Energy

The economic problem is a manifestation which comes out of a number of other problems. These are subjective in nature and constitute in their totality the lessons placed before the group and the challenge of growth which faces it. It can be resolved with effort and as the group consciousness. Each, as it manifests its own foci, comes into an understanding of the nature of the problem. Each one arrives at an understanding of his contribution to it. He can therefore correct his contribution so that it is a contribution to solution rather than problem. You understand that where the focus is brought into manifestation on the physical plane, there then, is the vehicle through which it is possible for the Hierarchy to function. As long as one polarity is in one place, center energies can be released, but center function cannot proceed. The objectification of the service potential cannot be achieved without center personnel through which to work.

The coming years will present all disciples both in the field and in the Ashram with great challenges so that all members of the World Group of disciples, wherever they function should be as ready as possible to serve humanity as disciples at the height or the maximum of their potential. This would mean that they would be serving where and how they were most needed and equipped to serve. It does not mean that the group would fail to function or to meet the needs of a demanding humanity if it were not functioning in one particular area. For that matter, the actual reason for the center location does not apply so much to you as it does to the Hierarchy. That is why we have said over and over again that from the Hierarchial vantage point the Rocky Mountain area is the best location for the center. Insofar as you as disciples are concerned, at this time and place it is not of as much importance as it is to the Hierarchy. It is a natural center within the devic life itself for the movement of the energy of synthesis and for the work, the service effort. It is the location which has been definitely determined for the Center of Synthesis for the world itself over a long, long period of time. That center does not have to be externalized or materialized until the end of the century. It does have to be by that time. By externalized, I mean in the sense of the same degree as the centers of Hierarchial force in the Himalayas. By the end of the century, the Rocky Mountain center in the United States does have to be in incarnation insofar as the Hierarchy is concerned. The Hierarchy must always account for conditions and circumstances which not only humanity but the serving disciples are manifesting.

Perhaps it would help you to consider what your physical service activities would be, as you take up center function. For then, if you include this in your subjective effort, you will be setting up that manifestation into which you will be working, individually and collectively. We come again to the basic, basic, basic problem of the group which does manifest outwardly in poor and unhealthy economy. That problem has to do with the inability of the members of the group to each establish your own right function in right relationship to each other. This has been the problem of the group from the beginning; it remains so today. There is still too much of the self in each one, so that he does not consider his function in relationship to other functions. He does not consider more adequately how his function relates with the other functions within the group. If each one is focused only upon his particular function and his particular activity without regard to the functions of the other members of the group, then he is not coordinating his activities properly. He does one of several things in his channeling of group energy. In the circulatory system of the group, if he is functioning in right relationship to everyone else's function, he aids in a right circulation and distribution of group energy and group life. If not, he may, on the one hand, divert some of that circulating energy, force, and substance from the group into wrong channels. Or he may constitute a block in the circulatory system of the group, which does not permit the energies to move freely through the etheric network or web of the group. He may constitute a block, either in the reception of energy or the distribution of energy as it moves into the center and as it moves out from the center, so that here are three ways in which he can affect the right circulation of group energy, force, and substance, and therefore effort, if he does not properly relate his function to the function of all other members of the group.

This has been a basic problem since the beginning of the group. Contained within it are certain other factors. Not only must he properly relate his function, but he must understand this function so that he can carry it out. He must know what it is he wants to do, how he is constituted to serve in the center and then put his own will, his attention and his effort into that direction.

Once this problem insofar as circulation of the life of the group is concerned, once this is resolved, the outer economic problems cannot manifest. They cannot be, because, remember, it has its causes in the subjective life of the group, not in the outer world in which you live. The outer life may appear to be the cause of the economic problem. It is the way you are relating to the subjective life of the group that causes it to be an economic problem. This you all realize to greater or lesser degree because this is the teaching you have accepted. This is the teaching to which you have responded. Therefore, you must realize that a problem is not the outer manifestation which it appears to be, but rather it is an inner condition, an inner problem, which has to be worked out within the self. Once it is worked out within the self, in right relationship to all others, then the outer problem disappears, for it has no cause, no basis, no fact in nature.

If you consider from the purely physical standpoint, what you will be doing in a center, what your activities will be, and relate each one from where he is now, his own particular state of consciousness, his responses upward and outward to Truth, his reaction, both of a positive and negative nature, then it should be possible for him, through imagery, through the use of his own imagination, by placing himself within that set of circumstances which the center itself will constitute and arrive at an understanding of his own problems and be able to work them out subjectively from above downward. Look ahead, but as you look ahead, look inside. Consider what the center will be doing. What will be its function? Then, as a natural result of that function, what will be its physical activities into which each one will be entering? Do not be concerned with the faults and defects of others, but place yourself within the situation and then work out, as you observe your own responses and reactions. Work out from above downward the manifestation of solution of the problem. Resolve that part of the problem which is your contribution. When enough of you have done this, then it will be possible for you to actually manifest the center function wherever you choose to manifest it.

Certainly it takes the effort of each one from within

Chapter 32

himself to bring about this solution. What are the physical conditions and circumstances and activities which will be necessitated by a center function? I am referring now to an actual center function, not probably what you would set up in another area. Because if you initiate the effort in another area, you will not consider it to be the permanent or the real center effort. It will be a matter of your getting together for meetings and of your carrying out whatever service activity you are able to squeeze into the effort. It will not be the same unless you make it so through a prevision, a preparing of the way.

The Disciple and Economy

272

Chapter 33

The Keys to the Door of Initiation

Economy as the Major Problem of Initiation,

A Mental Second Ray State of Being,

Lifting Above the Illusion of Lack,

The Bridge of Joy,

Harmony with the Laws of Nature

I am going to ask you to look upon the present situation, that is the present financial situation as it effects all of you, including its effect upon your group and upon other groups working under Hierarchial direction either consciously or unconsciously in their service to The Divine Plan for humanity. See this financial situation as a major opportunity insofar as this incarnation is concerned and take advantage of that opportunity by endeavoring to absorb the following information into your consciousness and to then utilize it in the coming months.

First, the major problem to be solved by humanity as a whole in its initiation during this cycle is the problem of economy. You realize that in the situation in which you find yourselves, you are not alone, but that you are one with every member of humanity, regardless of the amount of wealth he may or may not possess. That humanity in total and humanity individually is presented with this problem of economy as the major problem of initiation, spiritual initiation that is.

The Disciple and Economy

Realize that each member of humanity or every group within the body of humanity, solves the problem according to that level of consciousness of which he is a representative. So then the problem which faces you, while it is the same problem facing humanity, is none-the-less somewhat different insofar as its solution is concerned. You can resolve the problem of economy as it is related specifically to financial matters only through the use of different methods than the average person or group solves this same problem. Before you then, the problem, the understanding of it, has several different approaches. So then does the resolving of it have several different approaches, as there are various factors involved.

I am going to endeavor to give you a somewhat different understanding and therefore a different approach to a solution than you have had previously. This, however, does not mean that all of that which you have had is to be discarded or considered obsolete, but rather this new approach is to be included within the total, related to it and applied in right relationship to the other factors which you have considered previously.

But first, realize as completely as is possible that this problem facing you is not a problem which means in essence that you have failed or that there is anything wrong. It is not a problem which should give rise within yourselves to doubt. The greater the problem is or becomes, the greater should be your realization that solving this problem is a part of your service to that group of disciples within the world of which you are a part, regardless of what Ashram they may be functioning in or what organization they may be affiliated with. This constitutes a major part of your service to them, and it constitutes the major challenge, so to speak, of initiation insofar as you individually and collectively as a group unit are concerned.

Chapter 33

When the solution has been made manifest by your group unit or by any other, if it should come to that, working with the World Group of Disciples, the solution will have been, if not made manifest, at least brought into the realm of possibility and probability for all disciples functioning at that level of consciousness.

You have been given many points of instruction which constitute what is often referred to as occult hints, or clues, of a First Ray nature in the solving of this particular problem. It requires but a final push for you to reach and manifest the solution and that final push has to do with the incorporation into the brain consciousness of a certain state of being, of certain attitudes of a kind of understanding which will supersede the reactive patterns built into the etheric and therefore the physical instruments.

This state of being to which I refer will not negate other instruction which has been previously projected. You will still have to bring to bear upon intelligent substance the force of the will. You will still have to formulate planned activity and carry it out in order to be successful. But if you can bring into your brain consciousness these Second Ray concepts or ideas or states of being, then you will find the application of these other First Ray techniques which you have been given, much more easily achieved. The state of being to which I refer is so simple that it is constantly and continuously overlooked by disciples who are not basically Second Ray themselves. It is used by disciples functioning in astral bodies who are primarily evolving along Second Ray lines, but it is used in such a way as to clutter (if I may use this term) their sphere of influence with so much glamour that it is not effective in the area of economy and specifically of finance.

I am referring to a Second Ray state of being which is mental rather than astral, and yet which utilizes the tone, the force, the magnetic power of the astral body in such a way as to produce the sound and the sight of beauty, of harmony and therefore of abundance within the astral vehicle and from such use to materialize that abundance in the physical. Now to arrive at this without becoming caught up in the astral vehicle it is necessary for you to achieve a mental focus and then play the astral body as a musician plays an instrument.

A probationer disciple functioning, focused within his astral body, polarized there, would call this state of being one of faith but his faith would constitute to the mentally polarized disciple, so much glamour. And to the mentally polarized disciple of a First Ray nature – so much hogwash (if I may use one of your terms).

Life anywhere in any frequency range, whether it is physical, astral, mental or buddhic, can be and should be, and actually is to the initiate – an adventure. Every experience can be entered into with a kind of curiosity, (if I may use such a term), with a Divine indifference as to outcome, insofar as physical effects or manifestations are concerned, and yet at the same time with a curiosity, the kind which seeks to know. This is one attitude, one very necessary attitude which along with others makes up the state of being to which I refer, and it is an attitude which can only proceed from a mental focus.

Now at the same time, focused within the mind, within the body of intelligence which is one of the primary gifts that God or the One Life has bestowed upon man, it is possible to cognize the fullness – the fullness of all manifestation, and so, in that cognition, to lift one's sight above the illusion which is called lack, for such it is, a complete illusion. It requires as much energy, as much force and as much substance to manifest an apparent lack as it does to manifest an apparent fulfillment, and I would have you endeavor, at least, to realize this. Do not forget that the moment you descend

Chapter 33

from mental levels into the astral, the etheric and the physical, you become caught up in a world of opposites.

Fifty dollars must manifest its polar opposite, that is, it must be balanced by its polar opposite. The brain consciousness cannot contemplate one without the other, whether the other is submerged in the subconscious or not. Where one exists, so does its polar opposite. This is in these frequency levels. But begin to supersede the illusion by realizing that as much energy, force, and substance goes into the manifestation of one opposite as it does into the manifestation of the other. There is as much energy, force, and substance manifesting within nothing as opposed to $50.00 as there is within the $50.00. Or there is as much energy, force, and substance manifesting, going into the manifestation of a $50.00 debt as opposed to a $50.00 credit. Do you follow me? In other words, for all of you, whatever you manifest or are manifesting at this moment which you would identify as a lack (every seeming lack, need, unfulfilled, which you are at this moment manifesting), has required from you for its manifestation as much of an expenditure of energy, force, and substance as if you were manifesting its fulfillment. There is not in the whole of the One Life such a thing as lack. It is an utterly impossible concept. It does not belong any place. It has been created by humanity and it is a mis-creation. It is not lack – it is a definite manifestation.

All right then, in your mental focus, establish the attitude which can see the fullness of every manifestation – which can observe a tree, recognize the fullness of the manifestation of that tree, which can observe (and this is pure metaphysics), in a sense, a sandy beach and recognize the fullness of that manifestation, which can observe any form within the world of form and recognize the fullness of the manifestation – and then enter into a communion, a communication with that fullness. For you, in your human weaknesses, in being caught up

in the illusion of lack, you see lack about you everywhere from an astral focus within your brain consciousness. You see apparent lack in the manifestation of a
misdirected economy. You are tuned in to the vibratory
frequency of this manifestation and therefore direct
your energy, force, and substance both consciously and
unconsciously into it. You see it everywhere you look.
You see it in starving millions. You are misinterpreting
the reality, misinterpreting the very manifestation you
observe. And therefore you are manifesting within your
lives and affairs, that misinterpretation.

You see no $50.00. On the one hand you see $50.00 and
on the other hand you have no $50.00. In other words
the mind cannot conceive — the mind which is conditioned and controlled (now I am speaking of the physical brain consciousness) by the astral focus does not
perceive the reality. It perceives rather an illusion in
which polar opposites are manifesting. It cannot, therefore, conceive in that particular focus of any one without
also conceiving of at the same moment its opposite. And
this breeds fear. If you have, you are afraid you will not
have. If you do not have, you are afraid that you will
have and then will not have again. There is a constant
piling up of fear because of this illusion.

If you can work from above downward, you will begin to
see the $50.00 or the lack of $50.00, (the apparent lack
of it), the same way that you see everything else. In
other words, if you can get into that mental focus which
can observe the fullness of every manifestation, including the manifestation of apparent lack, which can see
the energy, force, and substance within that manifestation which knows, in other words, cognizes the power
which has gone into every manifestation, so that you
can begin to communicate, commune with that fullness.
Now, to commune with that fullness is not easy and yet
it is not difficult. It is not easy in that it requires one to
accept into his own heart that energy which manifests

Chapter 33

as joy, and for many this is difficult, because the moment that such a thing as joy is permitted entry into one's feeling experience, immediately guilt arises and fear, because of the polar opposites.

Joy is the bridge between the two. For instance if I can explain it to you, let us take an initiate, full blown initiate, as compared with one of you who are not yet initiate. Let us place the two in similar conditions. Take the initiate, place him in a strange city or country without apparently any means by which he can provide the necessities of living, and then consider yourselves, each in his own particular manifestation or situation. Now the initiate, contemplating his situation, would first experience joy; a joy which would communicate itself to every living thing near him or within the periphery of his awareness or contact. That joy would communicate itself to the ground or the street upon which he walks, to the grass or the trees or whatever vegetation was growing around him, to the buildings, to the animal life and to the human life, because his first natural cognition in that particular condition would be the fullness of life, the fullness of all manifest form. He would recognize this and communicate with joy that recognition to all of the devic life around him. He would not see, for instance, those negative manifestations in the world as dreadful, as manifestation of lack, but he would recognize what went into those manifestations. He would recognize the perfection of the devic life in its response to consciousness, as it manifests what the consciousness impresses upon it, and he would communicate this recognition. He would see no lack. This would be his state of being.

That attitude, that essential part of his being would then manifest a positive energy, a positive force, a positive direction of substantial or substantiating substance around him. There would be manifest no negativity within his instrument, no question. Because of this positive state of being, his mind would be free to cognize exactly what to do, how to do it. He would be able to bring the will to bear upon whatever intelligent activity were apropos and so he would manifest whatever fulfillments were required to the carrying out of his service. For instance, there is so much to be seen, so much to be cognized, recognized, simply in walking down a street or a road or looking out of the window. The fullness of life itself is everywhere about. There is so much beauty, so much harmony to be observed. And these are the building blocks of the initiate. These are as essential to him as are his will focus, his ability to direct will energy and his ability to formulate a planned activity and to carry it out. He uses his astral body as a musician uses his instrument, to produce that positive force which will manifest whatever he requires in his activities.

Five minutes of joyful communion with the devic life will do more than all of the years of an incarnation of worrying about a problem. To appreciate – appreciate the flight and the song of a bird – to appreciate the beauty that one sees all around, whether that beauty be man-made or whether it be created by nature is of no importance. But it is in the constant radiation of the positive magnetic force of the astral body by the man who is mentally focused that the whole being becomes so integrated that he can manifest only wholeness or completeness.

For instance, you might need or think you need – you might require such and such, an objective form, whether it be food, money, transportation, whatever it might be. This requirement should not blind you to the beauties of life, nor should it imprison you from the pleasures of living – the natural, the spiritual pleasures of simply living. And the man who is filled with joy will never go without. For nature works according to law. When you are filled with the knowledge, the cognition of

280

reality, then you are placing yourself in right relationship with everything you see and observe. You are not
influenced then by illusion. You are placing yourself in
right relationship with it. You see it for what it is.

The moment that you say this is good, then you are
accepting within your consciousness that something
else is bad, so you are caught in the illusion within the
reflected area between those polar opposites, and this
then is your magnetic field and hence your nature and
thus your manifestation.

You know, in theory at least, that everything that
manifests around you, everything which is your manifestation, every experience through which you pass, is
a reflection of your state of consciousness. Then if your
state of consciousness is that state of being to which I
referred, what can your reflection be, if you cognize
the fullness of all manifestation? If you are above
these pairs of opposites, if you can realize that the
pairs of opposites are only man's misinterpretation of
polarity and can lift above them so that your vibratory
frequency is in harmony with the laws of nature itself,
then your manifestation must reflect that state of
being. You can only manifest whatever your requirements are, because you are seeing all around you the
perfect manifestation.

There is only a communication of joy between you and
other people. You are placed in right relationship to
them. You see them for what they are, they have no
influence upon you because you are not imposing your
will upon any one else and his manifestation. They will
not change unless your relationship to the individual is
such that your recognition effects a change. In other
words, you are not going around changing the manifestations of the average individual but neither are you
being influenced by those manifestations.

The Disciple and Economy

Recognize that the famine stricken people of the world are putting as much energy, force, and substance into their manifestation as are those who are living in an opposite condition. It is not going to change the condition for the famine stricken unless that happens to be your field of service and you create or formulate whatever activity is necessary to effect a change for the purpose of evolving the consciousness – not feeding the people. You will be in but not of the world, actually.

You don't attract supply, you create it. Joy is one of the primary essences of life – be detached, divinely indifferent and yet curious, and above all an actor.

The soul manipulates the energy of mind or the mental plane. It manipulates the force of the astral and the substance of the etheric to produce a form in the physical or an appearance.

Joy is not an emotion, but it is like the bow of a violin when used upon the astral body and it will produce within the astral body that force which has its emotional counterpart of a positive nature which is a part of the manipulation of force, a part of the manipulation of the astral frequency. Joy is used to produce positive movement of force within the astral body.

So is beauty used in the same way – and harmony. These three will lift and bring into right relationship all of the frequencies of the astral body including any subconscious discordant tones. They are keys, particularly to the door of initiation.

I am going back to one of the major points which I intended to bring out in the beginning of this instruction, in the light of what I have said since. One of the major keys, the major points to be considered by you is the fact that the problem, which is a form, remember, filled with energy, force, and substance, is the major problem of the initiation which you are undertaking. It is, therefore, one of the greatest indications of your spiritual growth and development in manifestation. You have reason to be joyful when you observe the problem. So has humanity, if humanity could but recognize it. The problems of economy which so harass humanity today were not matters of concern to humanity a few centuries ago.

The problem will become much greater for the whole of humanity than it is now. As it becomes greater, the Hierarchy will rejoice, because this will mean that humanity is facing up to its initiation, and as it endeavors to resolve this problem and finally does resolve it, humanity will complete its initiation. Therefore we find nothing in the economic situation of the world to sadden or concern us.

Now I am going to proceed. Try to incorporate, try to become tuned into the attitude and to enter into it – be joyful. Take joy in the small, apparently small things of the moment. Enjoy the moment–by–moment living. Incorporate these attitudes into your state of being as completely as possible, and then proceed to resolve this apparent problem for the group. Do it, those of you who go out into the field, from a focus and function as the objective polarity in the world of affairs. Those who, because of their more apparent relative security, function as the subjective polarity, forming thereby a positive and negative polarity, functioning in the world for the purpose of resolving this particular problem for your group, if you can proceed with this focus, or from this focus, then you not only have my blessing and approval of any withdrawals from what you might call more esoteric activity, you have my urging that you do so.

It will be in achieving that you will become initiate, and one always becomes initiate by resolving a major problem not only for himself, but for all of those who are just within his level of development.

Now remember what I said at the onset of this instruction – what I have given you are Second Ray techniques, but they do not negate or supersede other techniques which you have been given previously. In other words it takes the combination of everything you have received to be successful. It will require the will focus, but if you can achieve this state of being which can cognize reality, then the will focus will be much more easily carried out, continued, than it would be from your usual state of being. And this applies to all of you.

Your purpose is service to humanity. Your goal during this cycle until you have manifested it, is a resolution of the problem of finance for your group effort which includes then the resolution of the problems of individual disciples wherever they may be of the group.

You who are not going out in the field are functioning as the subjective positive polarity because of your apparent relative security. Those who are going out in the field are forced to function objectively.

You see, you cannot contemplate one apparent positive without contemplating the other. The moment you say rich – you immediately consider this to be extremely bad. So a good must then have its bad.

You do need to decide. If you need a loaf of bread, certainly you plan to manifest that particular form and manifest it.

As I said, the individual who is astrally focused and who utilizes these Second Ray techniques in his lower frequencies, manifests glamour. He so clutters his whole magnetic field with glamour that he is not effective.

Chapter 33

The fulfillment of life, of nature – it is the nature of life to fulfill itself in form. It is all around you.

First achieve the attitude, the state of being to which I referred and your mind will be freed to cognize, to formulate whatever plans are the most apropos. There is a reason (there are many reasons) why some of you are forced into the objective role, a reason, as all reasons are, as a necessary part of growth in consciousness, a rounding out of your consciousness. Some of you have for so long moved along the First Ray impetus that you do not enter into the role of the actor in the world. You do not adequately communicate with people other than those who are at your level of development or close to it. You have forgotten how to play, and I am using this term deliberately. It is extremely important to your own development for you to recognize the value and the Divinity of all levels of consciousness, all levels of development – to be able to enter into a communication with these, to be able to so assume the role of the actor that it is as easy for you to play as it is easy for you to work.

Therefore I am going to tell you that a part of your success will come out of, directly out of, your entry into this type of experience. You will make contacts with people with whom you will meet and talk. Therefore I ask you to apply first this state of being to which I have referred, to the activity of communicating lightly as well as seriously, seriously only when you are called upon to do so, with all of those levels of development that you come into contact. This is important, for your isolation is a part, a major part, of the causal factor of the apparent lack manifesting in your life and affairs.

You have to learn to give yourselves to all of those with whom you come in contact rather than to withhold yourself. This tendency to withhold yourself from others has become greater since you have come into the relationship with one another, for you fulfill too easily, in a sense, one another's needs insofar as relationships are concerned and tend to withdraw further into your isolation from others. This hinders and delays you, and it could become a major block in your path of progress.

Index

Index

Index

law of right use, 191
Master Deva of, 190
mastered, 259
mind of Christ, 130
must come from, 173
new, based on, 45—
    block to, 47
state of consciousness, 50
none in agreement, 157
occult use, 195
of disciple, must manifest, 264
of One Life, 51, 68
of the One Life, 1
organization of energy, force,
    substance, 37
overshadowing, become
    receptive to, 50
potential, 34
present, utilize, 49
problem, solved, 259
will become greater, 283
problem of, 127, 273
problem solved, 166
problems in, 177
redirection, 71
reflected in group, 204
right use, 128
seventh ray, 45
spiritual understanding, 33
three basic laws, 191
we manifest that, 44
world, Divine Intervention, 257
wrong circulation, 71
Educational opportunities, 13
Elemental—
    opposition, 84
    forces, command over, 182
Embodiment, mastered, 72
Energies—
    on astral levels, 219
    thought-forms directing, 198
Energy—
    directed by mindwill, 198
    moves in straight line, 57
    one-pointed, 124
    receive and distribute, 216

wielding, 35
Energy, force, and substance, 21,
    45—
    directing, 72
    direct your, 278
    free movement, 177
    higher frequency, 127
    of One Life, 51
    outer activity, 55
    redirect, 66
    right assemblance, 64
    right direction, 66
Environment, real, 54
Equality, Principle of, 13
Equation, spirit with matter, 59
Esoteric sound, effect of
    consciousness, 55
Etheric—
    lines of light, 98
    network, externalizing, 117
    reactive patterns, 275
Evolution—
    long slow process, 200
    process of, 77
    supersede Soul, 122
Evolutionary process, self-
    initiated, 23
Externalization, goal of, 236

F

Faith, new kind, 200
Famine, 282
Father, The, 19
Fear, piling up of, 278—
    balance power of, 28
Fifth Kingdom, new law, 30
Fifth Ray—
    absorbing the essence, 225
    pouring in, 243
Finance, evocation for, 125
Finances, problem resolved, 207
First and Third Aspects, polarity, 66
First Aspect, movement into
    Third, 67
First Ray—
    downpour into etheric, 243

291

Index

Index

Index

Index

Index

The Disciple and Economy

Further Information

For further information on *The Disciple and Economy*, and related courses and materials, see:

www.wisdomimpressions.com

or write to us at:

WisImp@wisdomimpressions.com

or

Wisdom Impressions
P.O. Box 6457
Whittier, CA 90609–6457